NOTSO

Mumsy

murdoch books

Sydney | London

NOT SO
Mumsy

**Finding happiness, confidence
and your style in motherhood**

MARCIA LEONE

Contents

This book is dedicated
to all the mamas who are
searching for their village.

Motherhood is hard.
And it's beautiful. And it can
be both at the same time.

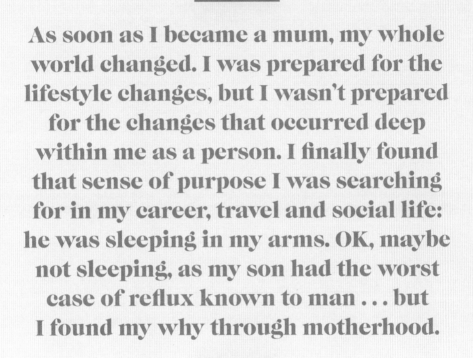

As soon as I became a mum, my whole world changed. I was prepared for the lifestyle changes, but I wasn't prepared for the changes that occurred deep within me as a person. I finally found that sense of purpose I was searching for in my career, travel and social life: he was sleeping in my arms. OK, maybe not sleeping, as my son had the worst case of reflux known to man . . . but I found my why through motherhood.

Not on a hill tribe trek along the Burmese border, not at a meditation retreat in the Panamanian jungle, not volunteering in South Africa or working in New York City, but in the domesticity of 'mum life'. In between the night feeds and tummy time, the relentless and the mundane—even the most challenging moments—was where I found my missing piece.

I didn't write this book just because I was offered a book deal. I wrote it because I had something to say. I wrote it in the shower; I wrote it in the car; I wrote it at 1 a.m., 2 a.m., 3 a.m. between the stop–start realities of mum life. Because after six years of sharing my motherhood journey and using my platform to share yours, I have learned that we don't need to be told what to do. Instead, we need to be told we are doing a good job. We need to share our experiences, while understanding that we'll find our own way through the unique experience that is motherhood.

This isn't a how-to advice book and I'm definitely no expert. I'm winging it, just like you, and I think that's the point. None of us really know what the heck we're doing—we are constantly learning and evolving; but we do need support. It does take a village, and I want this book to be yours.

I want you to walk away after reading this book feeling good about yourself and your choices—whatever they are. I want to normalise the parts of motherhood that have been hidden behind the facades of perfection and ease. I want you to laugh and feel supported, because you've got this! And sometimes you won't—but that's OK, too.

This is for the mum who struggled to conceive and the mum who fell pregnant at the first try; the mum who suffered a loss and the mum who has all her babies in her arms; the mum who breastfed and the mum who bottle-fed; the mum who 'bounced back' and the mum who didn't; the mum with a support team and the mum doing it alone; the mum who works out of home and the mum who works in the home. This is for the mum who is struggling to find herself in her new role. This is the book that I wish someone had given me while I was navigating this crazy new world.

This book is about finding yourself in motherhood.

I wish I could tell my pre-mama self that you don't have to tick off a list of things to do before you have kids. You don't have to cram in your 'best life'; you don't have to give up your identity. If I could go back in time, I would tell that girl working her nine-to-five that something bigger is in store. That it's OK she hasn't found her passion or purpose yet. That having a baby won't put an end to that search—it will actually ignite it.

I wish I could tell my pre-mama self that you don't have to tick off a list of things to do before you have kids. You don't have to cram in your 'best life'; you don't have to give up your identity. If I could go back in time, I would tell that girl working her nine-to-five that something bigger is in store. That it's OK she hasn't found her passion or purpose yet. That having a baby won't put an end to that search—it will actually ignite it.

Modern motherhood is finding the confidence to be who you want to be, not despite being a mother, but because you are one.

WHAT DOES 'NOT SO MUMSY' MEAN?

'Mumsy' is a British/Australian term used for mothers. The Oxford Dictionary defines it as 'giving an impression of dull domesticity; dowdy or unfashionable.' For me it's the notion that you lose yourself in or to motherhood. So, on the flip side, Not So Mumsy is for women who love and embrace motherhood, but who also want to retain a sense of self (and style or fashion or whatever they were into pre-kids). I think we all lose ourselves a little at some point in the early days—that's normal. Yes, you are a mum, but you are still you . . . maybe even a more evolved version.

WHO IS THE MODERN MAMA?

Motherhood has a new mood. It's edgy, powerful, honest and strong.

The modern-mama movement that began in online communities is starting to break the parenting glass ceiling when it comes to choosing a style that fits with your family and beliefs.

Modern motherhood is about respecting each other's choices. It's recognising we all do it differently, and that's OK. It's swapping slippers for heels as you dash out the door. It's building an empire from home in your pyjamas and a topknot. It's juggling like a pro one day and then locking yourself in the bathroom the next. It's deciding that you might want to dedicate yourself solely to being a mum.

It's navigating business meetings and leaking breasts, and rocking your favourite outfit with a bit of baby puke on your shirt. It's enjoying the fast-paced life or packing everything up for a simpler one. It's finding out your 'village' might be online.

It means adoring your baby, but admitting it's hard. It's putting everything into taking care of your kids, while keeping a bit for your soul. It's saying you were someone before being a mum, and that that person still matters.

It's about losing yourself, and then blossoming into a new version of you.

It's finding the confidence to be who you want to be. Not despite being a mother, but because you are one.

chapter one:
my story.

Many of you will have your own motherhood story . . . this is mine. There are so many experiences that have influenced the mother I have become; that encouraged me to start an online community, to share my story and give others a platform to share theirs. Many of these experiences were from my childhood.

I grew up in a large family on a rural property outside of Sydney in the 1980s. My father emigrated from Italy in the 1970s and became a well-known Sydney restaurateur—he actually opened up Sydney's first wine bar. My mother was a daughter of Italian immigrants and grew up in Sydney's inner suburbs.

I am the second oldest of six children. We went to a tiny country school, rode horses to our friend's place, helped Dad with the cows, rode motorbikes and had plenty of room to play.

I loved my childhood, but as soon as I became a teenager I felt stifled by the small town and wanted to get out and explore the world. At eighteen I went on my first overseas trip, and by nineteen I had moved to Bondi, where I was based for the next decade studying, travelling and working.

MY MAMA

I couldn't write a book about motherhood without sharing some insights about my own mother. She is my ultimate mama muse. Her motherhood story is as incredible as it is inspiring, and she has had such an impact on the person I am today.

Mum was born to be a mum. Growing up, she aspired to raise a big family and by twenty-eight she had given birth to six children. Over the next decade, when my youngest siblings were teenagers, she went on to foster and adopt six more children.

When I was seven years old, my younger sister Isabella died in a tragic accident. Watching my mother bury her child was beyond heartbreaking. This had a profound effect on our whole family. For my mum, I think this was the catalyst for her, years later, to decide to foster babies. I could fill this whole book with many chapters of my mother's story, but the one I will share is her struggle to adopt Angel (I have changed her name for privacy), a three-year-old girl from Kazakhstan. This story demonstrates the type of woman my mother is, and why she will forever be my inspiration.

Fifteen years after Isabella passed away, my foster sister, Zara, passed away at a similar age. After Zara's passing, Mum wanted to adopt a child in her memory. My aunt lives in America and forwarded on the details of an American agency that worked with orphanages in Kazakhstan and Russia.

When the agency asked what our family was looking for, Mum said she wanted the child most in need of finding a home. So the journey began to adopt a three-year-old girl who, because of her profound shyness, was deemed mentally unbalanced. If she didn't find a home by the time she was five, she would be moved to a mental institution (with adults).

Adoption into Australia is renowned for being near impossible at best, but my mum and aunt were assured by the agency that once the adoption was finalised in Kazakhstan, they would be able to obtain a visa for her from the Australian Embassy in Russia.

After three months of paperwork and preparation, my mum and dad went to Kazakhstan for a month to bond with Angel and process the adoption. When they arrived at the orphanage, Angel was brought into the room and told, 'This is your mama and papa.' Angel was incredibly shy, but after a few minutes she went up to hug her new mama. For three weeks Mum and Dad spent every day at the orphanage bonding with their new daughter. Mum said the orphanage was heartbreaking. It was incredibly rundown and filled wall-to-wall with cots and babies. She wanted to help more children.

Their fourth week in Kazakhstan was spent at court finalising the adoption and getting Angel's new birth certificate with our family name. She was officially part of our family.

My parents were advised to go to the Australian Embassy in Seoul to get Angel a visa as they were stopping over in Korea on the flight home.

Within a minute of being taken into a room in the immigration office, they were told they couldn't bring Angel into Australia. Mum asked the officer where she was meant to go and the officer told her she didn't care where she took her, as long as it wasn't Australia.

Mum informed the adoption agency and told them she had to return to Kazakhstan with Angel the next day. Dad flew home as my sister was looking after my younger siblings. Angel came down with a high fever and chickenpox during their overnight stay in a hotel. Mum felt totally alone and was crying in the hotel room as the sick little girl kissed her legs saying, 'Mama, Mama'.

Immigration in Almaty, Kazakhstan, was tough, but eventually they allowed Angel to be taken by the adoption agency back into the country. Mum needed to get back to her kids in Australia after being away for a month, so she made the heartbreaking decision to hand Angel back and fight for her from Australia. In retrospect, Mum said she should have flown to America with her, but instead she paid for her to live with one of the lovely adoption agency workers to ensure she didn't go back to the orphanage. It broke Mum's heart to leave her in Kazakhstan—Angel was so confused and was trying to run back to her. It was very traumatic for everyone.

Back at home, Mum sought legal advice and started lobbying the government to grant a visa for Angel. After three months, she knew she needed to get Angel out of Kazakhstan, and thankfully my aunt in America agreed to take her in until an Australian visa was granted. The adoption agency had to wait for an American couple adopting another child to come to Kazakhstan, so they could send Angel to America with them.

After nine months of what Mum said 'felt like being treated like a criminal for trying to save a child,' the Australian Minister for Immigration at the time gave approval to grant Angel a visa, as long as the Australian government's Department of Community Services (DOCS) were on board. Considering she was an approved DOCS foster carer, you would think this would be smooth sailing, right? Not quite.

After the whole family was interviewed and assessed by CatholicCare adoption services, it was decided our family could not adopt Angel because they felt we had 'adopted out of grief'.

My parents had to go through the court process of relinquishing Angel as parents and although they were heartbroken, they had some peace knowing that they had saved her from the orphanage. This situation was also extremely challenging for my aunt, who was left to find Angel a family in America. In the end she found Angel a wonderful family not far from where she lives.

Angel is now an extremely intelligent, happy twenty-year-old woman. She knows the story of how she found her family and has sent letters to my mum, thanking her for giving her a new life.

Despite the way that adoption panned out, my mum has no regrets. 'I gave her a life—even though it wasn't with our family, she is loved and happy,' Mum says on reflection of the experience.

Since then, Mum has fostered five children long term—each of them almost since birth. My foster brothers and sisters are now nine, ten, eleven, fourteen and eighteen years of age.

Not only did my mother raise twelve kids, but she did it with style and grace, too. I call her the original 'Not So Mumsy'. She gave everything to her children but also looked after herself. For her, that meant retaining her sense of style and competing in equestrian events. I remember her picking me up from our tiny country school wearing her leather skirt, oversized sunglasses and a bright red lip (it was the late eighties). She hadn't been anywhere fancy. She'd probably done the washing, prepared dinner and gone for a horse ride, but she always put in a little effort for school pickup because it made her feel good.

ISABELLA

My baby sister passed away when she was twenty months old. She was the same age my daughter is now and I was the same age as my son (seven). I watch my kids play (and fight) together—their bond is so strong that I just can't bear thinking of my son having to process a similar situation.

It was really hard to watch my mother grieve her daughter while I was trying to process what was happening as a seven-year-old girl. But truly understanding her loss as a mother myself has been even harder.

I remember the last time I saw Isabella alive. We were sitting in a circle playing a clapping game before school—all four of us siblings. It's as clear as day in my mind. The next time I saw her she was lying in a casket. I was told to kiss her on the forehead but I was scared. She felt cold and soft and hard at the same time. Her lips were blue.

Throughout the funeral service my mother wailed, 'My baby, my baby, my baby.' She had to be physically restrained from trying to get to her. It was so traumatic for everyone. Even the priest had to be consoled.

This happened in an era where you didn't 'talk about things'; there was no therapy or counselling. I kind of shut down and internalised my emotions. It wasn't until I became pregnant that I realised the profound impact Isabella's death has had on me.

Falling pregnant triggered anxieties I had around life, death, health and hospitals. All of a sudden, I had this fear of medical tests and doctors. I saw a kinesiologist who, after examining and testing my muscle responses, asked me, 'What happened when you were seven years old?' It was like a light bulb moment and it all made sense.

The day Isabella died, our family doctor picked us up from school. He drove us to the scene of my mother catatonic in bed, who delivered us the news. I had pushed this so far down into my subconscious that I had never processed what happened.

I found the responsibility of growing a baby pretty overwhelming. I was so happy and grateful throughout my pregnancy, but my fear of medical scenarios overshadowed what should have been an exciting, carefree time.

The impact of this childhood tragedy during my transition into motherhood really surprised me. It brought up anxieties and worries, but it also gave me the perspective to recognise what is truly important. It taught me to be grateful for the hard days, because even on the toughest days it could always be so much worse. It taught me that family and health are all that matter to me.

My daughter reminds me so much of Isabella. When I was struggling with fertility, I learned to meditate. In each meditation I would envisage walking down a set of stairs that opened up to a beautiful field. I would see this girl, a similar age to my late sister, and I would feel so happy and calm. I would watch her but I could never quite reach her. I used to think it was my sister, but now I know it was my daughter.

MY ENTRY INTO MOTHERHOOD

My memory of my son's birth is my happy place. I truly feel as though I was reborn the day he was born. My world changed in an instant. The rush of love and emotion was like nothing I had experienced. I felt like everything suddenly made sense.

It definitely didn't go as planned. I was induced, administered intravenous (IV) antibiotics and had a traumatising, very long second stage. But the moment I pulled that sweet boy onto my chest, I was in heaven. He rutted up my chest and latched on in his own time and we basked in our 'new family' glow.

My Story.

Twelve hours later our world was turned upside down. Within minutes of the midwife telling us she'd noticed bright green spit-up on our baby's blanket, he was whisked away to be poked at and prodded and passed from doctor to doctor for invasive scans. An hour later he was transferred to Sydney Children's Hospital's Neonatal Intensive Care Unit (NICU), placed in an incubator and hooked up to machines and IVs. I couldn't hold him and had to ask permission to touch him. I kept hearing our lactation consultant's voice in my head saying not to let anyone hold him for a few days so we could establish our bond. I stood by helplessly, my head spinning. I kept telling my husband through sobs that I just wanted him back in my belly. I had to fight every instinct not to scoop him up and run away. In hindsight they were probably working very swiftly to save his life, but at the time it was deeply frightening.

We were told our one-day-old baby needed emergency surgery for a malrotation of the bowel. I collapsed in tears and felt like I was having an out-of-body experience—looking at the scenario from above. Surely this could not be happening.

My memory of my son's birth is my happy place. I truly feel as though I was reborn the day he was born. My world changed in an instant. The rush of love and emotion was like nothing I had experienced. I felt like everything suddenly made sense.

He had surgery the next day. I convinced myself he wasn't going to make it. I told myself that my anxieties throughout pregnancy were valid. I kissed my baby goodbye before they took him to surgery, thinking it might be the last time I saw him.

I prayed and cried and ached to be with him. I yearned to comfort and hum to him like I did every day when he was in my tummy. While we were waiting to hear the outcome of the surgery, I sat in my room shaking while a nurse milked my breasts with her hands trying to get some colostrum for the baby.

I hadn't slept for 50 hours. I had come from the high of giving birth to handing my tiny baby to surgeons, unable to touch him or hold him. My world was spinning.

The surgery went well, but the recovery was long. The next three weeks were a blurry roller coaster of emotions. Exhilaration when we hit a milestone, and despair when we had a setback.

Our tiny baby wasn't able to receive any milk through the feeding tube for a week—he could only have clear fluid through an IV. His veins kept bursting and it would take three or four nurses to hold him down as they tried to find a new one. At one point, the only option left was his head. He was so hungry and I had to sit next to him with breasts exploding with milk. It was torture for us both.

I refused to go home without my baby, so after I was discharged we stayed at a hotel next to the hospital. I was by his side every minute I was allowed to be—to the point where the nurses were annoyed. Late at night my husband and I would play music to soothe him. His favourite was Crowded House's song 'Don't Dream It's Over'. He was nil by mouth for weeks, but after successfully establishing feeds, he was well enough to take home—a few days before Christmas. He was our miracle.

This was my entry into motherhood. Dramatic, right? It framed so much for me, though. The experience taught me about perspective, and gratitude. To not sweat the small stuff. Had I not had this experience, I don't think I would have coped with the transition to becoming a mum very well. The lack of sleep would have got to me. My son woke every 40 minutes, had severe reflux and could only sleep on me for months, but I was grateful for it all. My baby was alive and that was all that mattered.

FERTILITY

I know many of you reading this are already pregnant or have just welcomed your new bundle, but I couldn't write a book about motherhood without mentioning fertility, or infertility, as this has been such a huge part of my motherhood journey. Sharing my story while I was in the eye of the storm resonated with thousands of women around the world. It's what gave substance to my platform, and a voice to many. As much as I wished that it wasn't my story—it is. And it's my mission to tell it.

I never wanted to be the poster girl for fertility issues, but I was sharing everything else about motherhood and I would have felt like a fraud if I didn't share my experience of loss while I was in it. So I spoke about our family's struggles without knowing if we would get our happy ending.

We all know the miscarriage stats (one in four women under the age of thirty-five miscarry, as do one in three over thirty-five), but when the numbers are replaced with people, they take on a new meaning. The support I felt just knowing that others had been there and understood my experience was so helpful. This motivated me to continue to share. I wanted to acknowledge my babies had existed, so I spoke about them. Along the way I gave a voice to thousands of women who have gone through something similar. We are not alone—let us continue to share this burden by talking about our miscarriages.

No one has taught me more about life than this boy right here.

MY EXPERIENCES WITH LOSS

I carried you for all of your life and will love you for all of mine.

It's 2.54 a.m.; I'm in a hotel in Istanbul and I can't sleep. My hormones are crashing and I feel emotional. I can't believe it happened again. I don't want people to feel sorry for me; I don't want to be the poster girl for miscarriage. I just want to be a normal mum who can give her son a brother or sister. I don't know . . . maybe I should keep it quiet and pretend it never happened. But the truth is, it did. This is my story. And like it or not, I'm a 'mummy blogger'—and being a mum isn't all cute booties and designer prams. It can also be heartache and struggle and constantly doubting yourself.

I'm hoping my story will give a voice to others who are silently struggling with fertility. Women who scroll through their Instagram feeds full of beautiful bellies and babies and feel that desperate ache at the core of their soul. Women who feel like their body is failing them, who feel like they can't do what we are put on Earth to do. Yeah, it's tough. Beyond tough. Sometimes I sit in the car and scream at the top of my lungs. I have cried my way through spin classes and spent countless nights lying awake, wondering if I should keep trying to do this. It's taking a toll on my confidence. On my family . . .

If you had asked me a year ago, almost four months after our first miscarriage, I would have sworn we would have our second baby in our arms by now. I guess the universe had other plans. Over the past twenty months I have been patiently sitting on the sideline, watching friend after friend become pregnant, and scrolling through post after post of pregnancy announcements, growing bellies and bouncing babies. I picked the wrong line of work if I don't have a thick skin, right? To be honest, sometimes I do and sometimes I don't.

I still feel a longing when I watch those born at the same time my baby was due. My baby, whose heart I heard beating, whose room I had planned, who did exist—be it for less than three months and only in my belly. I loved that baby with a fierce protective mother's love and I grieved it as a mother who loses a child. I took my first miscarriage incredibly hard. It was beyond traumatic and completely unexpected after my easy pregnancy with my son. It took me three months of intense soul searching, meditation and therapy to heal and be ready to try again.

I was somehow prepared for my second loss. I was cautious and didn't allow myself to connect with the life inside of me. I was protecting myself from that intense grief and pain. It was still extremely sad, but I wasn't blindsided like I was with my first . . .

So here we are, finally in our first two-week wait since our last miscarriage. Can you believe this is the first month we have been able to try to conceive (TTC) since October last year?! The intrauterine insemination (IUI) was a little more full on than I anticipated. I was put on a drug to make me ovulate, which also made me crazy. I had to get bloods taken and have an internal ultrasound every two days, and give myself a trigger injection the night before. The procedure itself was painful and left me cramping and bleeding. Now the progesterone pessaries I take twice a day are giving me all the pregnancy symptoms, right down to the frequent urination, which in itself is a head f%$k. But I am so happy we can try to conceive! I know there is only a 25 per cent chance with IUI but we'll give it a few months of 100 per cent committed focus. I have slowed down on the work front, learned to say 'no' and to focus on my family because yes, you can have it all, but not all at once.

We're ready for you—mind, body and spirit—little one! I hope one day you get to read this story to know how much we fought for you.

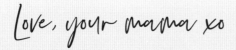

Love, your mama xo

A letter to my child

BY PHOEBE SHIELDS FROM P.S. IT'S A MUM THING

My darling,

We never did get to meet properly, did we? And yet, we were together for every moment of your life.

You slipped away from me, quickly and quietly, without making an impression on the world. No one even knew you were there, except your daddy and I. But you should know that you were loved. I like to think that you know that already.

I made a space for you in my heart.

But now that space is empty.

I have tried for years now to fill the hole you left. I thought, perhaps, when your brother was born he would take that space. But my heart grew and created a special spot just for him, and yours was left untouched.

Now my days are filled with the normal ups and downs of motherhood. My heart and mind are often consumed with loving and caring for your brother. The empty space you left is no longer at the forefront of my mind.

But sometimes, when it is quiet and the house is still, that empty space in my heart echoes so loudly that it can't be ignored. The hollow grief washes over me once more and I am stunned with the intensity of its power.

It seems that no matter what happens, or how much time passes, I cannot fill that void that you left.

So I have decided that I will leave that space in my heart exactly where it is. I will stop trying to fill it with other things, or pretend it isn't there.

It is your space and I am going to leave it just for you. I will carry you there always, in that space, in my heart.

Love, Mummy

BUT THERE IS HOPE . . .

I never anticipated I would be an 'IVF mum', especially after conceiving my son so easily. Secondary infertility, which is the inability to conceive or carry a baby after previously giving birth, is such a mind game. My internal dialogue was screaming: 'It's official. Your body can't do what it's supposed to. You're a failure!' It was such a mental hurdle for me to overcome, but my desire to have a sibling for my son was stronger, so I worked on my mind as well as my body to give us the best chance possible.

IVF is physically and emotionally exhausting. Daily injections, hormones, blood tests and scans, and really it boils down to a numbers game. Our issue was pregnancy loss rather than difficulty conceiving, so after two unsuccessful rounds of IUI, we decided IVF with preimplantation genetic diagnosis (PGD) testing would be our best option. They collected fifteen eggs. Eleven fertilised, nine made it to day three, five made it to day five, and then after the PGD testing, we were left with one viable embryo. ONE. And that little embryo is now my tutu-obsessed two-year-old daughter.

I shared my journey while I was still in it, not knowing the outcome. Talking about it turned out to be just as helpful for me as it was to others who were going through a similar situation. Even after I got my happy ending, I promised to continue to share this story; to never forget but to also give hope to those who may need it.

POST BY MARCIA @notsomumsy

THE DRESS

We have the loveliest cleaner who comes once a fortnight, and one particularly trying afternoon, I came home to find a tiny white dress hanging in my bedroom and a pair of baby girl overalls in the bathroom. She had seen the boxes of IVF meds and needles when she was cleaning and, even though we had never spoken of it, she left a note saying that in her culture, if you hang baby clothes around the house the baby will come . . . I can't tell you how many nights, weeks, months, years I lay in bed looking at that dress. It still hangs there—a constant reminder of how we wished for her. And here she is, our little angel, finally in our wishing dress.

POST BY MARCIA @notsomumsy

PINK BALLOON

As we turned off the busy highway into the IVF clinic on the day of our embryo transfer, a huge pink balloon literally came out of nowhere. It bounced between cars and landed on the windscreen of our car. My husband, who is not normally a universe/sign kinda guy, remarked, 'Well there you go, it's gonna be a girl!' . . .

At our twelve-week scan we were told the baby looked like a boy. In fact, they were 90 per cent sure it was a boy. At my next obstetrician appointment, she said the early scans are not necessarily correct, but she had the IVF results of the embryo and could confirm that we were having a girl! A few hours later she called me to tell me she was reading my sex, not the baby's! That's all I needed to realise we weren't meant to know. We didn't mind, so we decided, let's have a surprise. Throughout the pregnancy we would try and guess and I would say, 'But the scan showed . . .' and hubby would remind me of the pink balloon. What a moment it was when I pulled her onto my chest and finally saw that she was indeed my pink balloon.

I shared these two parts of our story on social media and they both went viral. I think that happened because they are messages of hope and that's what every mama riding the fertility roller coaster needs.

chapter two: pregnancy and preparing for a baby.

Those faint little lines on the pregnancy test change your life forever

I AM MAMA

Growing a human is exhausting. The crazy hormones, itchy skin, swollen feet, skin tags, heartburn, stretch marks, bleeding nose, 3579 toilet trips every night . . . but did I mention you are growing an actual human with eyes, a nose, lips and toes? Let's take a moment for that to sink in.

As soon as you see those little lines on the pregnancy test, your life changes forever. Pregnancy is such an exciting time, but it can also be overwhelming. There are so many physical, mental and emotional changes. Some women love pregnancy and others not so much.

Both of my pregnancies were similar physically, but emotionally and mentally they were worlds apart. I suffered anxiety before and throughout my first pregnancy. Just the concept of being directly responsible for the life inside of me was overwhelming.

Add the medical anxiety and fear of hospitals from the trauma I had as a child, and it wasn't the most relaxing time. I couldn't even get my blood pressure taken without having a panic attack. I was so grateful and excited and in love, but so scared something would go wrong. This meant that I couldn't fully enjoy the ride.

Despite experiencing two losses before my second full-term pregnancy, I was determined to relax and enjoy it. The meditation and self-care work I had done on my fertility journey meant I was in a much better place, but I still needed some extra tools and help in order to navigate my medical fears. Eight weeks into my pregnancy, I went to a hypnotherapist who gave me a meditation to listen to every day. It was absolutely life changing. During our two sessions, I thought there was no way it would work. She was just talking to me—and I was overanalysing, as usual—but, lo and behold, my medical anxiety was cured in weeks. By twenty weeks I was looking forward to my medical appointments and my blood pressure was as level and stable as they come.

BABY BRAIN

I read somewhere that a pregnant woman was joking with her partner about having two brains: her brain and the baby's brain. Unfortunately the reality for many of us is that while we do in fact have two brains, we've never felt so ditzy (no need to openly admit that, of course). I can't tell you the number of times I put ice cream in the pantry, laundry items in the fridge and stood at the front door wondering why my keyless car key wouldn't open my home. Forgetfulness, a lack of focus and difficulty remembering are common signs of 'baby brain'. Don't stress about it—everything is just as it should be!

BUMP STYLE 101

Thankfully maternity fashion has come a long way since mumu dresses and overalls, and there are plenty of creative ways to style your bump.

I invested in a few key maternity items, but for the most part I bought non-maternity, bump-friendly pieces that would take me through pregnancy, breastfeeding and beyond.

The key is to layer your clothing. Think a maxi dress and denim jacket, long vests, kimonos and ponchos. Some days I loved to show off my bump in form-fitting outfits, while other days I preferred oversized pieces paired with leggings.

These three staples will not only take you through your entire pregnancy, but are easy to mix, match and accessorise to create dozens of outfits for every occasion.

1. High-waist stretchy maternity skirt
2. Body-con maternity dress that holds you in all the right places
3. Good-quality, supportive and flattering maternity leggings.

Once you have these pregnancy-specific basics, you can pair them with tank tops, long-sleeve tees, oversized jumpers, long cardigans, blazers (great for concealing the baby bump in the early weeks), boots and sneakers to create many different looks.

Whether you're feeling like a glowing goddess or like you swallowed a doona (trust me, we all feel both!), the easiest way to bring a basic outfit to life is to add accessories. A textured jacket, oversized sunglasses and killer clutch will up your style game in a flash.

1

*BODY-CON
MATERNITY DRESS*

2

*HIGH-WAIST
STRETCHY MATERNITY
SKIRT*

3

*FLATTERING MATERNITY
LEGGINGS*

11 TIPS FOR
DRESSING THE BUMP

BY FREELANCE WRITER AND EDITOR JESSICA BOSCO

When you're pregnant, one of the hardest things (outside of, you know, being pregnant) can be dressing the bump. Finding clothes that fit, are comfortable and make you feel good all in one hit can be seriously tricky. Scrolling on Instagram, you look at pregnant women who seem to make it look so easy while you're over here feeling more like Homer Simpson than Blake Lively. But really, it's just a matter of finding what works for you. Embrace your new curves and changing shape with the help of a few simple tips and styling tricks.

1 Think outside of the maternity section. Don't rule out your favourite stores just because you're now pregnant; you might be able to size up in some styles and make them work with the bump.

2 Experiment with different looks. While some mamas are all about the body-con and showing off the bump, others are all about feeling floaty and free. Try on lots of things and find your personal maternity style—you might surprise yourself.

3 Invest in some quality items. Buy a few key pieces that can be mixed and matched.

4 Don't spend too much money on maternity-only pieces, unless you are planning on being pregnant a few times and they are quality, timeless pieces you will wear each time.

5 Buy with the option to return or exchange. You're still getting used to your new and changing body, so make sure you can return items if they don't fit right or if you don't like them later (especially if you are buying online).

6 Go shopping in your wardrobe. You may find that clothes you had tucked away in your wardrobe are speaking to you and your new shape. A loose-fitting dress that you once wore belted could now be perfect left loose and flowing.

7 Comfort is key. I can't stress this enough. If something doesn't fit quite right, is a little tight or annoys you in any way, don't buy it. (The same goes for your pre-pregnancy clothes. Don't keep squeezing into them.)

8 That said, you could buy belt extenders or belly bands to go over your jeans (or use the old hair-tie-through-the-buttonhole trick) so you can wear your favourite jeans that little bit longer. But once you finally make the move to maternity jeans, you'll wonder why you didn't do it sooner—elastic waistbands are everything!

9 Splurge on accessories. There's nothing quite like a new bag, shoes or some statement jewellery to take an outfit up a notch and you'll still be able to wear them when you're not pregnant.

10 Embrace the bump! This is the one time in your life where you can celebrate having a pregnant belly, so embrace the bump and have a little fun with your look. Your body is doing some pretty amazing things right now and it would be a shame to hide it.

11 Don't stress. If you just aren't feeling good in anything, don't worry. You won't be pregnant forever (even though it might feel that way . . .).

Finding your pregnancy style isn't just about your wardrobe. Yes, your body will go through some drastic changes, but so may your skin and, in turn, your beauty routine. I found the idea of what I should/shouldn't use in pregnancy so overwhelming. There is so much contradictory information—even among doctors and skin specialists. I chose to err on the side of caution and only use natural products (checking that all the natural ingredients were safe, too) and had everything signed off by my obstetrician. So for all the confused pregnant and future pregnant mamas, I have called in an expert to offer a definitive guide of what you should and shouldn't use on your skin.

PREGNANCY
SKIN CARE

BY PIPPA JAMES, A FACIALIST AND FOUNDER OF SKINBYPIPPAJAMES.COM

Growing a tiny human (and then going on to breastfeed that baby naturally if that's the case) has a major impact on how our skin looks and feels. Some of us are lucky enough to enjoy a pregnancy 'glow', while some of us can experience common pregnancy skin conditions like dryness and sensitivity, hormonal acne or melasma (the 'pregnancy mask'), and even some unexplained but harmless 'things' that just appear.

Many products on the market promote being safe for pregnancy and breastfeeding, but it's important to be sure of this claim. The best place to start is to understand the ingredients that are considered harmful due to either not enough research on their impact on the foetus or breastfed baby, or because the ingredients are known to cross the placenta and affect the baby.

We also need to consider that some natural products are not necessarily safe;

To prevent brown spots and skin discolouration during pregnancy, use sunscreen! Be mindful of choosing physical over chemical sunscreen, too.

there is evidence that some essential oils can cross the placenta and affect the baby, so you need to check 'natural' products, too.

The following ingredients can help combat common pregnancy skin conditions like acne, as well as offer skin-lightening or anti-ageing benefits, but are a bit too powerful for your growing baby.

Retinoid and vitamin A may be listed on ingredient labels as retinoic acid, retinyl palmitate, retinaldehyde, adapalene, tretinoin, tazarotene and isotretinoin.

Tetracycline, salicylic acid and benzoyl peroxide are commonly used in acne-fighting or anti-ageing skin care products and medication.

Some skin care brands, particularly cosmeceutical ranges, offer 'pregnancy-safe' vitamin A and retinol products, but you need to do your own due diligence. Check with your GP or obstetrician and decide what you're personally comfortable with using.

Hydroquinone is used as a skin-lightening agent in brightening serums and creams to treat conditions such as dark spots and melasma. It is tempting to use if you've developed dark spots but it's not worth the risk to your baby. To prevent brown spots and skin discolouration during pregnancy, just use sunscreen! Be mindful of choosing physical over chemical sunscreen during this time, too.

Look out for these chemicals in perfume and nail polishes: phthalates, formaldehyde and toluene. Use non-toxic nail polish brands instead.

Botox and fillers need to be avoided until after pregnancy and breastfeeding.

You also need to consider the potential effects of these essential oils found in many natural products: aniseed, angelica, basil, black pepper, camphor, cinnamon, chamomile, clary sage (often used safely during labour by midwives), clove, fennel, fir, ginger, horseradish (should not be used by anyone), jasmine, juniper, marjoram, mustard, mugwort (should not be used by anyone), myrrh, nutmeg, oregano, rosemary, sage, thyme and wintergreen.

SO WHAT CAN I USE?

Don't despair if the ingredients I've listed form the backbone of your anti-ageing skin care regimen. There are lots of highly effective ingredients that are safe to use while pregnant and post-partum.

Antioxidants and acids such as lactic acid, glycolic acid, vitamin C and azelaic acid are great options for pregnant women as they protect against UV rays, free radicals and environmental toxin damages. Vitamin C helps to repair environmental damage and increase collagen, while azelaic acid helps with hormonal acne and hyperpigmentation, all of which can be issues during pregnancy.

The final word is to always ask your GP or obstetrician if you are using anything you are unsure about.

PREPARING FOR BABY: KEY ITEMS YOU NEED

When it comes to setting up a nursery, most first-time mums (including myself) go a little overboard . . . and rightly so—this is exciting! But a few months in, you'll probably realise you don't need a lot of the stuff you bought. The second time around I didn't even set up a nursery until the baby was almost six months old, which speaks volumes as to what you really need.

It's always a good idea to wait until your baby is born to buy the big investment pieces. That way, you can see what you really need. I realised pretty early on that the big, old, ugly glider chair was a back-saver for me and Mr 'will only sleep on Mum's chest for three months.' We didn't really have much use for the change table, so the second time around we put a change topper on our chest of drawers and it was a great space saver. As with everything in this new-mum world, what works for one mum and baby may not work for the other.

Impulse buys when you've had no sleep during the first three months are also probably not a great idea. I think I bought every miracle sleep apparatus on the market that promised to settle my baby. In the end I didn't use any of them—he just wanted me! When it comes to baby clothes, buy one or two nice outfits for photos or special occasions, but the reality is they'll live (and poo and vomit) in their onesies, so save the pretty outfits for after four to five months.

POST-PARTUM PLAN

We spend so much time preparing for the birth with classes, exercise and research, but the birth is such a small part of motherhood and it's usually over in one day. That's not to say it isn't the most exciting and important day of your life, but we also need to focus on what comes next. Creating a post-partum plan will allow you and your partner to discuss changes that will occur once you become new parents, and give you the opportunity to put plans into place to make your transition into parenthood much smoother.

CONVERSATIONS WITH PREGNANT WOMEN

What you shouldn't say
to a pregnant woman

* You look further along than …
* You look tiny!
* Are you sure you're not having twins?
* You're carrying low/high, that means …
* My labour was 75 hours long and I wanted to die the entire time—I'm sure yours will be fine though!
* Better sleep now/see a movie/read a book/go out for dinner (subtext: get prepared for your life to suck).

What you should say
to a pregnant woman

Three simple words: YOU. LOOK. GREAT.

It works for post-partum women, too.
Oh, and pretty much everyone else. Good vibes only!

chapter three: birth.

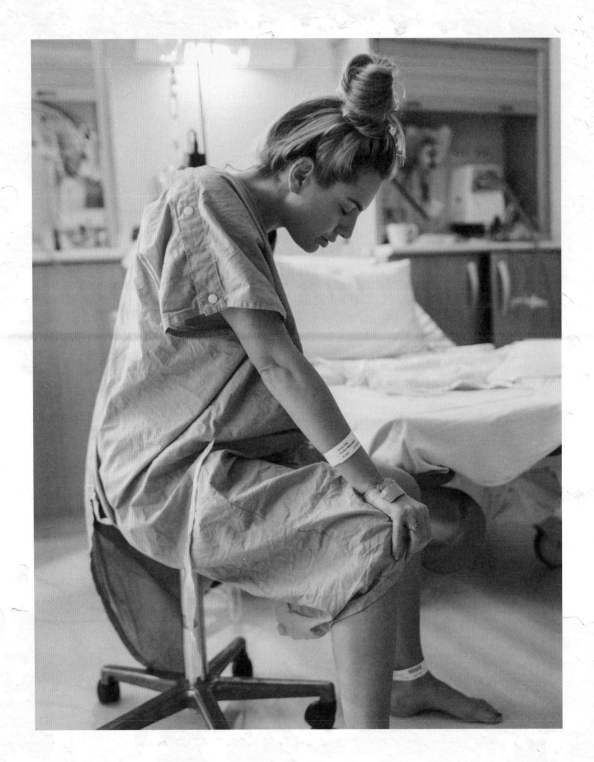

Welcoming a baby into the world will no doubt be one of the most incredible experiences of your lifetime. There are wonderful classes, techniques, books and support groups available to prepare physically, mentally and emotionally for the birth, so I'm not going to focus too much on that topic. Other than to say it is just as important to focus on a post-partum plan. The birth will (hopefully) last just one day, whereas motherhood lasts a lifetime.

Most of us have a vision for how we would like our birthing experience to go, but births don't always go to plan. While it's important to have a plan, it's best to be a little flexible about it. Know your birthing rights, ask questions and educate yourself on the different scenarios. But don't forget to place trust in your caregivers.

I used the Calmbirth method with my first pregnancy. We spent a beautiful weekend away learning all sorts of techniques—many focused on partner involvement with touch and back rubbing. Well, I can tell you when I was in real labour, the last thing I wanted was to be touched. Every time my partner rubbed my back I felt pain like an electric shock run through my body.

I had a pretty specific birth plan, but I also had an open mind. So when my plan was thrown out the window because I had to get induced (couldn't walk around, sit on balls, shower, etc.), we adapted a few things so I could bring elements of that plan into the delivery. I managed to pull both of my babies out and onto my chest, which were such powerful moments. I was also aiming for a drug-free birth with my son, but after hours of contractions, I just wasn't dilating and it wasn't until I had the epidural that I dilated from 1 to 10 centimetres within an hour. So the moral of the story is I was glad I had a plan, but just as glad I had an open mind. A healthy baby and a healthy mum is really the end game, so whatever it takes is whatever it takes.

I also want to mention that if you had a traumatic birth and it continues to affect you, don't be afraid to ask for help.

Know your birthing rights, ask questions and educate yourself on the different scenarios. But don't forget to place trust in your caregivers.

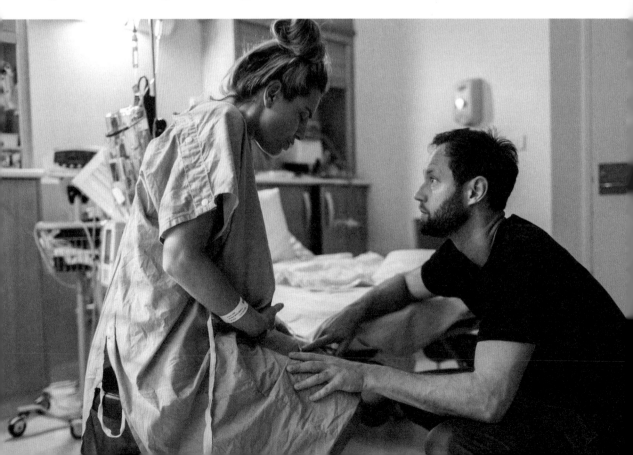

THE HOSPITAL BAG

There is so much around our birth we can't control, but one thing we can do is create a beautiful birthing environment. It is really nice to bring things to make us feel organised and calm, so here is a packing list that can help you on your way.

BIRTH

Pack a separate bag just for the birthing suite so you don't have to search through your bigger bag.

* birth plan (printed out)
* essential oils
* diffuser
* playlist and small speakers
* comfy robe
* stretchy bra
* magazines
* swimwear (if you're having a water birth)
* toiletries (see far right)

MAMA

* 2 comfy pyjama sets with a super-elastic waist
* 1 nightdress with buttons
* 5 pairs large comfortable undies (dark colour)
* 1 pair tracksuit pants or stretchy pants
* 1 robe
* 1 oversized T-shirt
* 1 nursing tank
* 1 dress to go home in or take pictures in (something that makes you feel pretty)
* 2 maternity bras
* pack of maternity pads or adult nappies
* slippers or socks
* pack of breast pads
* nipple shields
* water squirter or bottle (for your lady parts)

BABY

* newborn nappies
* 2 swaddles (soft and ideally organic)
* 1 pack water wipes
* 2 newborn onesies
* 3 newborn singlets
* booties and a beanie
* burp cloths
* dummies (just in case)

TOILETRIES

* cleansing face wipes
* lip balm
* face moisturiser
* concealer, bronzer and mascara
* nipple balm
* toothbrush and toothpaste
* hair ties and bobby pins
* hand sanitiser
* dry shampoo
* hair-brush
* deodorant
* body wash
* travel-size shampoo and conditioner

SHE'S HERE! THE BIRTH OF
OUR RAINBOW BABE

The night before our babe was born, my son and I had a lounge room dance party and hubby and I finalised our name shortlist. I went to bed excited but also really sad that it was the last night I'd be woken by those little tummy kicks and somersaults. I really loved my pregnancy and I was mourning the fact that it could be the last time I'd experience the miracle of growing a baby.

I had been 4 centimetres dilated for weeks, walking around with what felt like a bowling ball between my legs, so when my obstetrician recommended we book in to break my waters at thirty-nine weeks, I was relieved.

The next morning we arrived at the hospital and spent some time with my son before my mum picked him up. He ate all the jelly, raised havoc with the midwives, gave the belly and I some big cuddles and then I tearfully kissed him goodbye. It was the last time it would be just the three of us.

At 10 a.m. the midwife attempted to break my waters in the hope I would go into spontaneous labour. OH EM GEE . . . I remember the pain from having them broken with my son, but this was next level. Of course I got the midwife with the self-proclaimed shortest, stubbiest fingers, and because my cervix was still posterior (ideally it needs to be more anterior for labour), the fingers and hook were having a hard time getting in. Three attempts and so much blood and pain later, I found myself inhaling the gas like my life depended on it, while the midwife went to search for the nurse with the longest fingers. Thankfully she was able to break them at the first go—even though she said the baby might have a scratch on its head!

I spent the next hour or so standing up in the bath holding onto my husband as gushes of fluid escaped my body. What a crazy feeling! There is certainly no dignity in walking around wetting the floor and having your husband clean up after you!

Mild contractions started a while later, but not at the level they were expecting so they gave me some syntocinon (oxytocin) to get things moving. Even though I knew I wanted an epidural (I had a third-degree episiotomy [incision] with my son and knew I would need another with the scar tissue), it was important for me to go through as far as I could without it. I wanted to really feel the contractions.

A few hours later I had the epidural, which totally shifted the mood in the room. I'm not sure if it was the drug or the experience itself, which was pretty full on and scary. I was told, 'Whatever you do, don't move at all'. After hours of contractions I was still only 4 centimetres dilated; my excitement was replaced with anxiety, uncontrollable shaking and a really flat feeling. This lasted for a couple of hours.

The epidural had changed so much since I had my son. Back then, I had not been able to feel anything during my son's birth (which I'm sure resulted in the three-hour traumatic second stage). This time, I could feel the contractions, just not the intense pain. I went from 4 to 10 centimetres quite quickly and easily, and as soon as I was told I would be able to start pushing in the next 20 minutes, my mood lifted and the excitement came back.

In my second birth, it made the world of difference to feel when I needed to push. My husband was my only support person this time and he stayed up at the right end (strict instructions from me!). The poor guy didn't know whether I wanted him to breathe with me or be my punching bag. All I know is that I squeezed the eff out of his hand!

Just before the second stage, the midwives changed over and the very same midwife that delivered my son came into the room. I couldn't believe it. What were the chances that five-and-a-half years later in a major Sydney hospital, I would have the same midwife! I took it as a positive sign that I was ready to do this.

A few pushes in I knew the standard position on my back wasn't going to work. They lowered my bottom half so it was more like a squat, but I didn't feel like I could push the baby down. As soon as I moved to a side position I could feel the baby coming down. After three pushes, the doctor said she could see the head and there was a mass of dark hair. This was the motivation I needed to breathe her down. All that work in meditation and visualisation helped me so much. The doctor said with the next push I could reach down and pull my baby out and up onto my chest. She also said she wouldn't tell me the sex so I could see for myself.

I mustered everything I had with that final push. As I reached down, I was overwhelmed with emotion and started crying as I pulled her onto my chest. Yes, her! I couldn't tell the sex at first because of the umbilical cord. I was looking for a little 'doodle', as my son would say, and looked up at my husband in utter shock. 'It's a girl?!' We had been told she was a boy at the eleven-week scan, even though we didn't ask to find out. We also didn't ask for confirmation at later scans because we wanted a surprise.

Nine months earlier, on our way to the IVF clinic to have our only embryo put in, we pulled off a busy highway into the clinic car park and a huge pink balloon came out of nowhere and landed on our windscreen. 'Well, that's our sign,' said my husband (who is not usually a universe-sign kind of guy). Throughout this pregnancy we kept referring to that pink balloon we'd seen months before. And when I pulled my pink balloon onto my chest, the joy, the emotion, the heartache and the relief were overwhelming to feel. She was here. And she had a great set of lungs.

We had two names shortlisted if it was a girl, but as soon as I saw her, I knew.

The medical staff were surprised at how small she was—none of us expected a 2.8-kilogram baby! My son had weighed almost 4 kilograms, and at our thirty-four-week scan she was already measuring 2.8 kilograms. After I delivered the placenta the doctor noticed that it was split, which she said probably was the reason my daughter was so small. But she was healthy and beautiful and perfect. As I was stitched up she got straight onto the breast and suckled like a champion.

After my traumatic experience with my son, where he'd been taken away within 24 hours for emergency surgery, the midwives and doctors were determined to give me the birth, care and experience that I missed out on with my son. And they did. It was wonderful.

POST BY MARCIA @notsomumsy

AFTER BIRTH

I'm 40 hours post-partum. I've had zero hours' sleep; my body feels like it's been hit by a bus. I'm walking like a rhinestone cowboy and Zooper Dooper ice blocks are my new BFF—although I'm sure I will never eat one again. My organs are figuring out where they live, the after-birth pains are rivalling the contractions, the sign on the door is guiding me through my first post-birth poo and my milk just came in. Forgot about that little (big, swollen) chestnut—hello night sweats and shredded nipples . . . BUT LOOK! I made a wee human! A little lady, no less! I stand here in absolute awe of a woman's body and what it's capable of. I am so proud. Seriously, we need to be worshipped! #imadeababy #hospitalselfie

Those first few days in the hospital are such a blur. The emotions are so real, and so overwhelming. The love is like no other, but the anxiety can also be at an all-time high. I mean, where is the handbook?

We never got that beautiful experience with my son because he was moved to the NICU. I mourned that for a long time. We didn't get to have our family come and visit and show off our new baby. Instead, we were thrown into this situation where we couldn't pick up our baby and had to hand him over for surgery and recovery. When visiting hours ended I had to go back to the other side of the hospital and then a nearby hotel without him. It was torture.

Whatever your birth experience, one thing is universal: the moment a child is born, so is a mother.

My experience the second time around was beautiful, but it came with a different set of anxieties—worrying about my other child. My husband had to be home with him so I was alone with the new baby for the first few days. I forgot how overwhelming it could be. On the third night my milk came in and it upset her tiny tummy. She was in so much pain that she screamed the entire night. I remember shaking in the bathroom on the verge of a panic attack. I hadn't slept for days and thought, *I can't do this*. I was googling 'night nannies' and wondering if I could stretch my credit card to pay for one. I felt so overwhelmed. I thought I would never be able to sleep again.

At the same time I felt immense guilt for even thinking these things. Every day for three years I had pined for her and now that I had her—I kind of wanted to send her back! That was day three. It was rough. The hormone crash, the lack of sleep, the new world. Thankfully, the next day, after a few 40-minute catnaps and a wonderful nurse who did her best to settle my daughter, I felt a little better. I was excited to go home, but of course I still felt a little anxious for the next few weeks to roll out.

Whatever your birth experience, one thing is universal: the moment a child is born, so is a mother. When you lock eyes with your child for the first time, your life is simply changed forever. And nothing can quite prepare you for it.

At some point you
are going to feel
that you cannot do it

. . . but you can.
Trust the way it is
meant to happen for you.

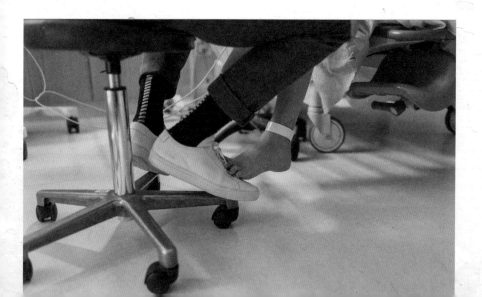

Birth.

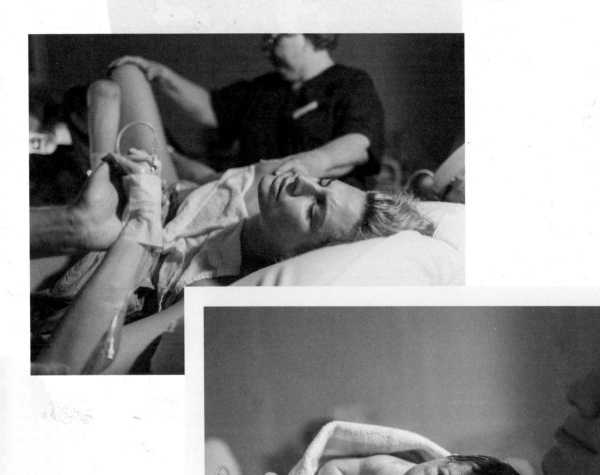

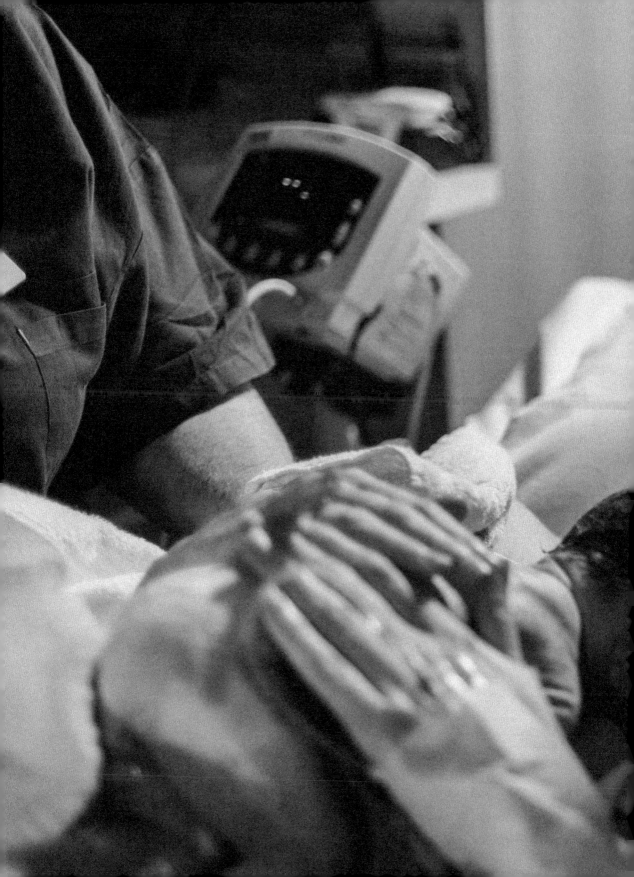

When you lock eyes with your child for the first time, your life is simply changed forever. And nothing can quite prepare you for it.

A CAESAREAN IS NOT
THE EASY WAY OUT

BY NOT SO MUMSY CONTRIBUTOR RACHELLE ROWLINGS

This is for 21-year-old Roman . . .

I kept having the same daydream. I was at a deli, I requested some shaved ham and then they asked what part of my body they should take it from. That was me—feeling like a deli meat, potentially now a vegan and lying motionless on a cold, sterile operating table.

I'd gone from assuming I'd deliver in a room not dissimilar to one in Cedars-Sinai, with a couple of hearty pushes and a cold flannel dabbing my forehead to being dressed like a human condom, breathing deeply and bending forwards while they inserted a lamp post into my spine.

To add insult to injury, I'd had to tan my 39-week 'Mum-bum' because my anaesthetist was a Calvin Klein model! I was terrified and full of resentment.

Why couldn't my body, this magical body that had made, cooked and carried a healthy baby, deliver naturally? Why did my son have to have his head against my spine and why was my pelvis too small?!

Did I fight for it enough? Should I have tried harder? Did my $7000 obstetrician just want a scheduled delivery so he could hit the first tee by 9 a.m.?!

Right up until the moment my legs went numb, I was disappointed in myself. A hasty, uncomfortable four minutes later and we were parents.

Ten fingers, ten toes, one little penis and here was our boy. Eyes fused shut, covered in what looked like fish batter and the closest thing I've ever seen to perfect. He, this magical being, was the easiest part of the following five days.

I had wished that I were stronger. I had wished that motherhood could have instantly toughened me. I had wished that the intense love for my son would make me numb to the pain. But it didn't!

I'd describe my emotional state as when the song 'Wind Beneath My Wings' plays in the film *Beaches*. My mental state was like a convenience store slushie. My will to live was low. I loved my son and I appreciated this healthy, beautiful baby, but I was broken.

Birth.

I hated the drugs that were being forced down my throat hourly, but without them I was in agony. I hated that I couldn't stand, sit or function without someone helping me.

I'd always been so independent. Now, I was like that browning pot plant you tried so hard to take care of but it somehow still died. I was sure my husband was going to throw me out and buy a new one. Especially after he had to help me to the toilet each day, change my 'surfboard pads' and endure my catastrophic emotional assaults on him!

After a fairly feral fungal infection, an allergic reaction to the hospital tights (strange, I know), excess fluid around my spine and my pert Cs being eaten by gravel rash EEs, we were on our way home.

It was a terrifying, lonely, agonising six-week recovery.

I'm not that Queensland vegan yogi who, three days later, was healed and back doing headstands. I was that whingey, anaemic, antisocial train wreck that went into complete hibernation.

I ignored calls and watched too many episodes of *Botched* while trying not to drown my son with the excess milk I was blessed with. I may have eaten a worrying amount of cheese toasties.

I'd fear a cough, be terrified of a sneeze and once considered weeing into a cup so I didn't have to squat on the toilet. It was real, it was raw and it was all I had to think about during the long days of my new human sausage laying motionless on my chest.

I remember thinking that I would become agoraphobic. That I would use salad tongs to reach for things for the rest of my life. And that my only form of exercise would be walking to the fridge! If it weren't for the love of my husband, the strength of my family and my desire to be the best mum I could be to my son, then I would have let it defeat me.

Each day got a little better. Each day I gained a little more belief in myself. Each *Botched* episode made me realise that it could be worse. A lot worse! I could have contracted a flesh-eating bacteria after having a $60 boob job in Guatemala. It was just a caesarean, for goodness sake!

So I went for a walk to the end of the street. Then to the end of the block. Then to the bakery. And then I stopped looking back. My body still loved me—it was still strong, agile and young—and it was fighting for me to love it back.

This pot plant just needed some water, some sunshine and to be told that even though it was a little limp, discoloured and droopy, it was still pretty!

Nearly twelve months on and I am running and box jumping, and spinning my 11-kilogram burrito in the air. Would I do it again? Over and over if it meant I could cuddle my son, smell his glorious smell, listen to that infectious giggle and hold his little hand as he conquers the world.

My body did that. And I couldn't be more proud!

chapter four: the newborn bubble.

A letter to you

Hey there new mama,

   I just want to let you know you are doing a good job. Whether you're in a bubble of bliss or a bubble of hell (or a mixture of both), you're doing a good job.

   If you haven't left the house in days because the last time you tried it took six hours, three changes and a badly timed nap only to get vomited on when you walked out the door, you're doing a good job. If you haven't been able to go to the bathroom, let alone make a cup of tea because the baby will only sleep on your chest, you're doing a good job. If your newborn grows out of those gorgeous itty-bitty clothes before you get a chance to put them on, because surviving the day in a nappy and a singlet is all you can manage, you are doing a good job. If you find yourself googling 'night nanny' and wondering if you have to mortgage the house to hire one, you're doing a good job.

   If you're feeling resentful, isolated, teary and bone-weary, just know these blurry groundhog days won't last forever. You will feel like yourself again, maybe even a stronger version, and one day you will look back and give anything to be trapped under that squirmy screaming baby, even if it's just for a minute . . .

Marcia xo

Those newborn days . . . for some this time is the most beautiful cocoon of love ever experienced; for others it's the most overwhelming shock to the system. For most, it's a combination of both.

After our touch-and-go start with my son and our fertility struggles to conceive my daughter, I was sure I had the overarching perspective to get me through the tough times, but sleep deprivation and hormone fluctuations do not discriminate. Add the monotony and isolation of those early days and it can be a slippery slope to anxiety and depression.

The hardest part for me wasn't the first few weeks; it was when my hubby went back to work. When friends and family stopped checking in and the surreal new baby excitement settled down. Everything went back to 'normal'—except for us. This wasn't my 'normal'. This was a whole new life. How did I go from running campaigns and coordinating my outfits to googling poo colour and logging which breast I fed from

last? The days felt long. I was so in love and so happy but simultaneously overwhelmed with the monotony.

I remember sitting on my feeding chair for the best part of twelve weeks as one day rolled into the next—watching the clock until Daddy came home. I would stare at the doorknob and would literally jump up and pass him the baby as soon as he walked in. Not every day was a struggle, though, and sometimes only part of the day was. When they say it's a roller coaster, they mean it.

A baby meme was floating around when I was in the newborn bubble, which summed up my experience perfectly: 'I love you so much my darling, but the second your father comes home I'm gonna bust out of here like I'm escaping Alcatraz.' I'm sure every new mama can relate to that feeling.

POST-PARTUM DOULA

Everyone wants to hold the baby, but who holds the mother? I wish I had known about post-partum doulas when I had my babies. I didn't have any family help with either child, and this was something I really struggled with. All I wanted was someone to drop by with some nutritious meals and watch the baby while I had a long, hot shower in peace. (Without the phantom cries!)

A post-partum doula's role is to mother the mother, offering emotional and practical support to new parents. I truly think it's something we all need.

There is a reason this newborn phase is called the 'fourth trimester'. I feel this concept relates to mothers just as much as babies. After nourishing, growing and connecting with our babes on the inside, it can take time to adjust to the new world after you give birth. Give yourself time. Feeling overwhelmed is normal, but it's also important to understand when you may need help—don't be afraid to ask for it. You've got this. And if you don't, there are some great places you can turn to for help.

FRIENDLY REMINDERS FOR NEW MAMAS

* Drink plenty of water.
* Do your pelvic floor exercises.
* Buy a nice pair of pyjamas—you will be in them a lot.
* If you haven't had an adult conversation for a while, call your mum or a friend, or go to a cafe and order a coffee.
* Stand outside on some grass when you feel overwhelmed.
* Take a few minutes just for you each day—a shower in peace or a cup of tea in the sun can make the world of difference.
* If you're able to, book something just for you once a week that makes you feel good—a blow-dry, facial, massage.
* Order in food. Don't worry about cooking every day.
* Ask for help. If someone wants to visit, ask them to bring lunch.
* LAUGH—watch a funny show, film or video.
* Remind yourself that you've got this!

ADJUSTING TO *PARENTHOOD*

BY NICOLE HIGHET, FOUNDER AND EXECUTIVE DIRECTOR OF
THE CENTRE OF PERINATAL EXCELLENCE (COPE), AUSTRALIA'S PEAK BODY
IN PERINATAL (PRE- AND POST-NATAL) EMOTIONAL AND MENTAL HEALTH

Adjusting to parenthood and life with a newborn brings with it lots of change.

Learning new skills and adjusting to a new lifestyle and routines can take lots of energy—and sometimes this will be energy you simply don't feel like you have.

Your baby may or may not be the baby that you expected to have. Some babies will be very settled, while others will take time to settle and may cry a lot, which demands from you both great patience and commitment. This can be especially the case if your baby has health problems like colic or reflux, which can cause them to be particularly unsettled.

It is a time when things can feel overwhelming. You may have times when things feel out of control. You may have fleeting doubts as you find yourself constantly learning and adapting in the first few weeks of your baby's life.

Most people find the first six to eight weeks with a new baby the hardest. While people may not openly discuss many of the challenges in these early weeks of parenthood (if at all), there are a number of common hurdles you may face throughout this time. The greatest challenges that parents commonly experience in their first few weeks of parenthood include:

* **Recovering from birth**—particularly if it was traumatic or you were highly dissatisfied with the quality of care you received.
* **Breastfeeding**—it may come easily to you or it may be yet another challenge, and it may be different to what you had expected or hoped for.
* **Lack of sleep**—this can greatly affect your mood, energy, patience and ability to think clearly.
* **Feeling overly emotional**—this can be compounded by a lack of sleep and feeling that things are out of control.
* **Coping with an unsettled baby**— babies all come with their own unique temperaments, which can place additional demands on your patience

and feelings towards your baby.

* **Bonding with your baby**—for lots of reasons, it may take longer than you expected to develop a connection with your baby.

* **Body image**—with pregnancy and birth come changes to the way that women may look and feel physically, and the new lifestyle as a parent can also influence their bodies. This in turn can have an impact on their self-esteem and body image.

* **Managing priorities**—finding time for everything while also meeting the needs of your baby may mean you need to let some things go for a while.

* **Managing advice from others**—endless advice can leave you questioning yourself and your capabilities, so trust yourself as the expert on your baby.

* **Relationship dynamics with your partner**—your relationship with your partner is constantly changing as you accommodate the baby and adjust to life.

* **Relationship dynamics with your family**—not only are your expectations of parenthood likely to be adjusting, but so too are those of family and friends. You'll begin to see where and how everyone fits into the new picture.

These are common challenges faced by many mothers and fathers, yet new parents often don't seek practical and/or emotional help early on. When this is the case, the impact of these challenges can build up over time, placing you, your partner and baby under even greater stress.

It's important to remember that these issues are common and, with help, they can be mastered. Alternatives can also be found to help you cope and reduce your level of distress.

If you are expecting or have recently had a baby, you can sign up to receive free fortnightly information to guide, support and reassure you throughout pregnancy and early parenthood at cope.org.au/readytocope.

With pregnancy and birth come changes to the way that women may look and feel physically, and the new lifestyle as a parent can also influence our bodies.

THE FIRST OUTING

It's always a big milestone the first time you take your baby out. We had a couple of doozies. The first was 'swaddle gate'. I'm going to begin by saying that I'm not sure who thought a 1500-metre origami fabric wrap would be a good idea for sleep-deprived parents and a screaming baby. After close to two hours of wrapping said baby and myself into a pretzel-like cocoon, we finally nailed it. I got organised and just as we were about to walk outside, I felt my son's body go limp. We freaked out, checked his breathing and got so worried that I unwrapped him and poked him to wake up. Turns out he was just sleeping—which was the reason we wanted to swaddle him in the first place!

Then there was the trip to the baby store, because clearly the 4567 trips before bub arrived weren't enough! We were on the hunt for some sort of magic sleeping apparatus. My husband jumped out of the car at the same time as me, and the doors automatically locked—with the keys and the baby still inside the car. I was that screaming banshee mother flagging down cars, trying to break the window. Thankfully we had some help to break open the boot. Back home we went, without any magic sleeping apparatus and I vowed not to leave the house for another month.

My first solo attempt was just as adventure-filled. Our maiden lap of Westfield ended abruptly with projectile vomit on the David Jones counter, a hysterical baby and what felt like 75 pairs of eyes on me in a lift, topped off with an emergency breastfeed in the car. Safe to say I waited a fair few weeks before venturing out again.

With baby number two you don't have the luxury of staying at home. Depending on the age gap between your children, you might be thrown into the time trial of school drop-offs, pickups and nap times. Thankfully I didn't have any major mishaps, just that time I dropped my son off at school with my pants inside out and a shower cap on the back of my head—but he got there on time and I had obviously showered, so I count that as a huge win.

In all seriousness, I found my groove after about six weeks, and by twelve weeks I felt like I (kind of) knew what was happening. I lived for my coffee dates with Mum and friends a couple of times a week. Sometimes you just need to debrief about poo and swap birth stories with someone who is in the same stage of parenting as you.

BODY

Not only are you adjusting to a new little person, you are adjusting to a new you—mentally and physically. I am not going to talk too much about physical changes in the first few months, except to say this: if someone walked up to you and handed you the most life-changing, precious gift you could ever receive, how would you feel about them? How would you treat them? Talk to them? Well, your body just did that. It grew a human being with eye-lashes, chubby fingers and a beating heart—be kind to yourself, mama.

Your body has changed for a reason. The fat stores, the swollen breasts—they all have a purpose. Talk to your body with respect. Praise it like you would praise your children.

Spend those first few months getting to know the new little human you just created. Take this time to focus on the miracle of what your body has done. Take a great-quality supplement, go outside, stand on the grass and take a deep breath whenever you need to, and be grateful. The best way to love yourself and your new-mum body is to eat nourishing foods to give you energy, help you heal and keep your mood stable. Do your pelvic floor exercises; go for a gentle walk outside each day and bond with your baby. Take the pressure off. There's plenty of time for 'fitspo', if you so wish, in a couple of months' time.

STYLE TIPS FOR THE IN-BETWEEN BODY

After months of dressing a bump, it can be tricky to then have to style your new post-partum body. There are so many factors to consider. Your body shape will continue to change for months. If you're breastfeeding, you need clothes that provide easy access and feel comfortable for you and your baby, but you want to look and feel nice, too.

Thankfully we have moved past 'maternity wear' to 'bump-friendly fashion', which are pieces that can be worn throughout pregnancy and beyond. Keep your pregnancy favourites—all those stretchy and flowy options can be perfect go-to pieces post-baby.

Don't let anyone tell you leggings aren't real pants! Post-partum leggings are a staple—they sit comfortably high and can help your tummy recover by keeping it supported. Faux leather or real leather leggings are great options when you want to be a little more dressed up, too. An added bonus is that they're wipeable.

Invest in some mix-and-match basics. T-shirts and jumpers are fine for breastfeeding—just make sure they're oversized and lift up for easy access. If you are wearing high-waisted pants, nothing is revealed and the T-shirt can double as a cover—as can a long cardigan or kaftan. Keep your staples basic and update them with accessories if you are going out or want to feel more put together.

Try not to focus on your old wardrobe—especially 'milestone outfits'. Move all of your pre-baby clothes into storage or a different section of your closet. You can revisit them, if you want to, a few months later.

SLEEP WHEN THE BABY SLEEPS . . . FOLD LAUNDRY WHEN THE BABY FOLDS LAUNDRY

It is completely normal for your baby to wake every two to three hours in the early days. If 'Betty' from mothers' group's baby is sleeping through at ten weeks, just know this is not the norm.

Remember, it's only a 'sleep problem' if it's a problem for you. If your mental state is at risk or you have to go back to work, speak to an expert about the gentle techniques that can help. You aren't doing anything wrong if your baby or you need extra assistance.

Get into a routine if that helps you feel in control. If you find it puts too much pressure on you, then go with the flow. Take in their newborn smell as you feed them to sleep and rock them to sleep. They were in your belly for nine months and they just want to be close to you. It won't last forever, mama.

How can you ever
say anything negative
about your body
after you have felt
the dancing of life
from inside your womb?

— AMETHYST JOY

11 THINGS EVERY
NEW MUM SHOULD KNOW

BY LAUREN HEFFERNAN, A CERTIFIED HOLISTIC MATERNITY AND CHILD SLEEP
CONSULTANT, CERTIFIED SLEEP EDUCATOR AND THE FOUNDER
OF ISLA-GRACE. W: ISLAGRACE.CA; IG: @ISLAGRACESLEEP

I find there is a common concern among new mothers. They are all so worried they are not doing the right things, that they are creating bad habits, that they don't want their babies to be dependent on them to go to sleep, that they will never be able to sleep on their own if they let them sleep in their bed with them, that they are failing their child in some way.

I really cannot tell you how much this breaks my heart. Some women have babies with reflux, some have colicky babies and some have amazing little sleepers but they don't even know it because another mum told them that their baby slept through the night at two months.

I am writing to all of the incredible women who are doing the best job tending to their baby's needs. For some, this means surviving hours and hours of crying as they are too worried to give their baby a soother because someone told them it was a 'negative sleep association' to go to sleep while sucking.

So for all of you amazing women who are somewhere within these first crazy six months, this is for you. Here are my eleven tips for the first six months of motherhood.

1 YOU WILL MAKE THE BEST DECISIONS FOR YOUR BABY.

This is because you are their mother. Do not listen to what anyone tells you about sleep (or anything else for that matter). Please believe that trusting your gut is always going to lead you to make the right decisions. You are not failing them. If you are feeding them, changing them, loving them and getting them at least a basic amount of sleep, then you are doing great! The more you stress about 'not doing the right thing' because you are reading articles about 'baby sleep' on the internet or reading about other mums in a Facebook group, the more you are taking the joy out of the time that you do have with your baby. I absolutely love this quote by co-sleeping expert James McKenna:

'Do what works for your family and trust yourself to know your baby better than any external authority. You are spending the most time with your baby, and every baby is different. Infants, children and their parents intersect in all kinds of diverse ways. Indeed, there is no template for any relationship we develop. When it comes to sleeping arrangements, many families develop and exhibit very fluid notions of where their baby "should" sleep. Parents with less rigid ideas about how and where their babies should sleep are generally much happier and far less likely to be disappointed when their children cannot perform the way they are "supposed to" — i.e. sleep through the night.'

When it comes time for your baby to sleep, your number one job as a mother is to teach them that sleep is a pleasant place to go and a safe place to remain. If you are trying to force them to sleep (because you read in a book that their wake window was meant to be 45 minutes) and they are not tired, you are teaching them that sleep is stressful. Your baby mirrors back all of your emotions. If you are frustrated, they will be frustrated. Follow your instincts; trust your gut and you will always know what to do.

2 DO WHATEVER YOU HAVE TO DO TO GET THEM TO SLEEP.
It is really important not to get caught up in too many sleeping dos and don'ts for the first few months. For the first three months especially, you really only need to be feeding them, changing them and putting them back down to sleep. For those of you with fussy/extremely alert/high-needs/reflux babies, you know so well that sleep is a challenge—do whatever you have to do!

3 THERE ARE NO 'NEGATIVE SLEEP ASSOCIATIONS' . . .
Nothing is wrong with co-sleeping/breastfeeding to sleep/using a pacifier, etc. Please breastfeed your baby to sleep, please use a pacifier (once breastfeeding has been established) if that helps, please rock your four-month-old to sleep if it helps them to relax, please use the carrier or the stroller and walk your baby to sleep. Yes, I am a sleep coach and I am telling you to do all the things you heard were 'bad' or 'negative'. This is how babies want to go to sleep. Eventually they will learn to do it on their own, but for now, help them . . . they are so young and little.

I always hear this term, 'negative sleep association', and it frustrates me. We all have associations with going to sleep. We may use white noise, we may read a book, we may have a specific set of sheets we like and some people even look at their phones before bed (this one is really not great for your melatonin production, though). There is nothing negative about needing something to help you relax into sleep.

If you aren't planning on staying in your baby's room, and they don't know that you leave and come back, it is more than fair that they have an association with going to sleep. If they have a particular association that you are not enjoying, remember that you are the one that built that association into the routine, which means you are also the one who can take it out and replace it with something else.

When rocking your baby to sleep is no longer something you want to do because it is taking an hour, then change it (if it is taking that long then it is likely not working for them, either). Yes, this will be met with some resistance but if you are gentle about the transition and give your little one time to adjust, then the resistance will be minimal.

If your child loves sleeping on you during the day and it is no longer working for you because there are things you would like to do (like have a shower—a luxury no first-time mother thought she would go days without), then maybe let them fall asleep on you and work on the transfer. Wait until they are in a deep sleep (their body will eventually go limp and they will stop twitching and moving), and try putting them in the bassinet (feet first) by slowly laying them down. This can remove the feeling of falling that can sometimes wake them up.

4 IF YOUR BABY IS WAKING EVERY THREE HOURS AT NIGHT THEY ARE NORMAL!

Newborns have two sleep states: active sleep (which is similar to adults' REM sleep) and quiet sleep (which is similar to our non-REM sleep). We now know that active sleep is necessary in order to keep babies from dying of sudden infant death syndrome (SIDS). Babies spend more time in active sleep from 2 to 6 a.m. During this time, they are much more likely to wake if they are hungry, cold, wet or not breathing (which again, is so important).

Their sleep cycles are actually shorter than ours (lasting only 50 to 60 minutes), and therefore they can experience a partial arousal every hour or so. There is a biological reason for the waking: it is for survival. In order for children to grow, they need to eat and therefore need to wake up to eat. If a child is too cold or too hot, they need to wake up in order to let their mum know. If a child isn't breathing, they need to wake up. Anything that forces a child to sleep too deep, too soon is dangerous.

Active sleep also has other benefits. It is thought to be 'smart sleep' because the brain isn't resting; it increases the blood flow to the brain and is thought to be responsible for more rapid brain growth. The point of this rant is that children should be waking at night—it's necessary for their survival.

5 KEEP YOUR BABY CLOSE.

This is true both at night and during the day. There is such a push to have babies in their own sleep space, but it is important to note that room sharing is recommended for the first six to twelve months in order to reduce the risk of SIDS. There is absolutely no need to rush your baby into their own crib in their own room. If they are still waking several times at night and you are exhausted — co-sleep (I am not allowed to promote bed sharing, so, by co-sleeping, I mean room sharing). You will get the extra sleep you need, and your baby will get the closeness they love. As I mentioned above, there is nothing wrong with this. I promise that if you co-sleep, your child will still be able to go to school on their own and will grow up to be a strong, independent person.

Keeping your baby close during the day is also important. If they want to nap on you . . . go for it! They are babies — they want to be close. I cannot tell you how many women I work with who don't hold their babies for more than an hour a day because they are worried that they are 'spoiling' them. You cannot spoil a baby by snuggling them. Really look at the amount of time you are holding them. It is easy to get caught up in the daily tasks (diaper changes, tummy time, swings, toys, etc.), and when you really look at the total amount of time you spend holding them on any given day, it is often very little. They need this closeness and if you can keep the contact skin-to-skin you will be satisfying their need for closeness.

Remember that in order for a child to become independent, they must first be securely attached. Babies need physical proximity. They need to sense the person they are attached to through smell, sight and sound. Their needs can be summarised as proximity, protection, predictability and play. They also need a parent to respond sensitively and consistently when they signal. The biggest predictor of how well a child turns out is that they have a secure relationship with at least one primary caregiver.

I think the biggest frustration around keeping babies close comes down to two factors. Firstly, that expectations don't meet reality. If someone prepared us prenatally for what life would look like after having a baby, I think we would be a lot more open to accepting the first year. If you knew that you would be up all night parenting, that your baby would spend all day sleeping on you or near you, that you were not going to have time to clean the house or do laundry and that it would be really hard, then you wouldn't be so frustrated when this became your reality. No one tells you how isolating it feels to be home all day with a baby glued to your chest.

Secondly, our culture no longer supports the new mother. We don't have the village and the tribe that once helped a mother raise her baby. More and more women are expected to do it all without any help. Some families I have met have the mother working part-time in the first year while still trying to meet the needs of her baby and keep a clean home and put a meal on the table. Some of my clients in the United States are going back to work after three months and trying to find a way to pump enough milk for their baby, find childcare for their baby and then manage all of the emotions that come with being separated from their baby.

Social media can also be unfriendly to new mums. We see pictures of perfectly put-together mums just hours after having a baby. This is not the norm. I highly recommend staying away from social media and 'Doctor Google' in the first year. It is important for a mother to find her own way through without feeling pressure from others to do something that doesn't feel right. It is hard enough to get through the first year, but constantly comparing your baby to others, or your life to the picture-perfect Instagram-mum, is enough to take all the joy out of being a mother to a new baby. Instead, find online groups where you can vent and share your sleep challenges among an amazing and supportive group of families.

6 CONNECT WITH AN IBCLC.
If you plan to breastfeed, it is so important to make sure you find someone who can support your

breastfeeding goals, such as an International Board Certified Lactation Consultant (IBCLC). Make sure they are listening and that you are clear about how you are feeling throughout the process.

If you are feeling exhausted and it is no longer working for you, then let them help. If you feel like you can't do it anymore, then tell them to support you while you stop. Breastfeeding relates to sleep as well. Within the first three months of breastfeeding, your supply is hormonally driven. After three months, it is based on how many times your breasts are being emptied. If your baby gives you longer stretches at night and you are missing those feeds, this impacts on your supply. If you are feeding on a schedule, this impacts on your supply. If your baby is distracted during the day and not eating as much, this impacts on your supply. If your baby is waking up several times at night and eating, they might be doing their job—keeping up your supply.

Your body produces more milk at night because your prolactin (the hormone related to breast milk) levels are higher. If your baby is distracted during the day or if you have started them on solids early and are using these as a meal (please ask your lactation consultant about this), then your baby will eat more at night. This is because it is dark, the snuggles are nice and the milk comes more easily.

NB: You must see a lactation consultant if your baby has colic or reflux. They will help you to figure out why your baby is 'colicky' or why the baby has reflux. They will look at your latch, your let-down, help to look for food allergies, etc. Use this resource.

7 AVOID OVERSTIMULATION.

It is so easy to forget that babies are so little and that everything is so new to them. Moving into a new room is a crazy experience for a one-month-old baby. Looking out the window is very stimulating. Going on a walk is stimulating all of the baby's senses—new noises, new smells, new things to see—even the outside air tastes different.

We often forget all of this and slip into the role of 'director of amusement', needing to stimulate our babies with toys all day. I see so many mums with bright plastic toys attached to their babies' strollers—why? Looking at a tree is new, listening to the birds is new, hearing a dog bark is new. A toy can actually be too much stimulation.

If a baby cries and turns away from a toy on a play mat, we can feel like they are bored of it and need something else. But maybe, just maybe, they are exhausted and overstimulated and need to just look at your face or move into a quiet, dark place to wind down. I am talking about this because our daily activities impact on sleep. A trip to the grocery store right before a nap might make for one very overstimulated baby, so give them a longer wind-down if you want them to nap.

8 TAKE A LOOK AT YOUR SLEEP ENVIRONMENT.

This is a really big one for new babies. You want to make sure that the environment is perfect. If it is too hot, your baby will not want to sleep. If it smells like cleaning products or any other strong scent, your baby's sleep might be interrupted. If you are turning on a night-light to change a diaper, your baby may not want to go back to sleep. If your child is highly sensitive and their pyjamas are itchy or have tags, or the detergent you are using is bothering their skin, then these could all impact on their sleep. If your house is noisy around bedtime, consider a white noise machine. Another question to ask yourself is, 'Is the air dry?' The right environment is really key to a good sleep.

9 USE MOTION NAPS FOR SLEEP.

Put your baby in a swing, use a carrier, go on a car ride (the car seat is not a safe place for a child to sleep so please transfer them when you get out of the car) or get them into the stroller. Babies love motion naps and they should be your go-to method if your baby just won't sleep. Motion is really good for brain development.

Have a look at your lifestyle. Do you like to get out of the house? Do you like to hike or walk as a family? If you do, you will want your baby to get used to sleeping in the stroller or in the carrier. Again, don't worry that they will never sleep in their crib.

Most babies that I work with before the age of six months need at least one motion nap a day, and it is rare to see a baby at this age taking all of their naps in the crib. Some babies before six months want nothing to do with naps in the crib and this is also OK. Switch up your naps—maybe you snuggle for a nap, use the carrier for a nap and get out in the stroller for another nap.

One of my clients was joking with me the other day about how she has lost all of her baby weight because she had a reflux baby and needed to walk him in the stroller to get him to sleep. Her and her husband have been laughing because it is the one and only good thing for them about reflux.

Motion naps are amazing for getting the last nap of the day, as it is often a hard one to get. Also, 30-minute naps for the first five months are completely normal and are enough. Motion naps will help you get these catnaps. Your baby might take eight 30-minute catnaps in the day and that is fine.

10 LOOK FOR THE SMALL SUCCESSES.

It is really important not to focus so much on the bigger picture when it comes to life with a newborn. Maybe you got them to sleep in the swing for twenty minutes so you could take a shower (HUGE). Maybe they took a pacifier and looked comfortable for a few minutes (HUGE). Maybe you found a great overnight diaper and they didn't poo through their sleeper (again, HUGE).

11 MOST IMPORTANTLY, TAKE CARE OF YOURSELF.

Please do things for you and ask for help. It is so important to take a walk or get a coffee or enjoy a glass of wine. Ask your parents or your partner to help, even if it is only for an hour. Your baby may cry because you aren't there, but if your child is in the arms of someone who loves them, and you need an hour to yourself, they are absolutely fine to cry and be supported. It is important that you are in a good headspace when you are with a newborn baby.

You cannot take care of your baby if you do not take care of yourself. We do self-care for our children and our family. We come back in a better headspace and are more patient and understanding when we have taken care of ourselves. You also do not want to model self-sacrificing behaviour, as they need to know the importance of caring for themselves.

Don't worry if your baby misses a nap in their crib because you want to get out of the house and meet a friend—enjoy yourself.

It is really important to know that a lack of sleep and hours of crying has been known to trigger some forms of post-partum depression in women. Please don't be ashamed or embarrassed to seek help.

You are doing a wonderful job. You are the absolute best person to be caring for your baby. The first six months are so hard. Hang in there, don't be afraid to ask for help and make sure you take time for YOU.

The newborn bubble.

HILARIOUS CONFESSIONS FROM SLEEP-DEPRIVED MAMAS

We say kids do the funniest things, but they've got nothing on sleep-deprived parents! After two-and-a-half years of interrupted sleep, I know a thing or two about the whacky things that happen when sleep doesn't. But putting nappy cream on my toothbrush is child's play compared to the confessions from these exhausted new mums.

'I was in the living room watching TV, and as I looked around the room, I realised that I saw only one of my one-month-old twins. After nervously glancing in all directions, I asked my husband if he could see the other twin. He looked at me kind of funny and said, "He's attached to your left breast."'

'I tried to attach the dog lead to my son while trying to take him to school.'

'As I was giving my four-month-old son a bath, I started to panic—his little feet were green! After a moment, I realised I was so exhausted that I never took off his [green] socks!'

'I started making my daughter's bottle—with a tea bag, milk and sugar! It was a cracking cuppa.'

'I answered the phone, and then started walking around muttering that I couldn't find my phone. The person I was on the phone with pointed out that I was talking on it. I hung up and went back to bed.'

'I got dressed in my pyjamas and went to bed. After realising I left the lounge room light on, I got up and got dressed in my "day clothes" to go and turn the light off. I didn't realise my mistake until I got back to bed but was too tired to change again, so I just went to bed fully dressed.'

'I went to get into the car and forgot I still had my toddler on my back in a carrier.'

'I woke up in the middle of the night to my baby crying and started patting his bum back to sleep . . . only to realise I hadn't got out of bed yet and was actually patting my husband's bum.'

'I went to the supermarket to quickly get some bread and was rocking and patting the bottom of the bread like it was my baby.'

'I sat down and started peeing with my underwear still on.'

ARE THEY A 'GOOD' BABY?

This really has to be one of the silliest things we say to new parents. All babies are 'good' babies—some just need a little extra TLC. I've had a waking-every-40-minutes, unsettled reflux baby and a waking-every-three-hours 'easy' baby . . . both were 'good' babies. For some strange reason, we measure 'goodness' with sleep. It's silly, really. When someone asks if your baby is 'good', they are really asking, 'Do they sleep well?' 'Do they cry?' 'Are they fussy?' Basically, do they disrupt your life as little as possible? Even though the person asking the question is usually well-meaning, it puts pressure on parents and expectations on babies. Of course your baby is 'good'! I'm yet to meet a 'bad' one.

chapter five: breastfeeding 101.

Many new mums or soon-to-be mums find breastfeeding to be the most challenging or intimidating part of early motherhood. Not only is it physically demanding, it's also emotionally demanding and comes with its own fears, expectations and judgements.

We are told 'breast is best' and undeniably, it is. Scientifically, nutritionally and emotionally—even the backs of formula tins agree. But for the most part, we aren't given the practical and consistent support to make it work, which adds so much pressure for new mums. On the flip side, after six months to a year of breastfeeding, we are told (in Western society) we shouldn't feed for so long. In fact, 40 per cent of women say they stop breastfeeding because of societal pressure. So unless you fit into this 'timeline', chances are you are going to feel judged for how you feed your baby.

I nursed both of my children for two years, and the reason why I am so passionate about breastfeeding education is because of my own experience with my son. Our breastfeeding journey didn't start off easily. In fact, it started with a midwife literally milking me for my colostrum, as my baby was in the NICU unable to even receive milk via a tube.

I didn't know how long I wanted to nurse for, but I knew I wanted to try. I saw a lactation consultant while I was pregnant, who told me how important the first few days were for bonding. Unfortunately we didn't get that opportunity to bond as my baby was whisked away from me. It took weeks before I could hold him for more than a few minutes at a time, let alone try and feed him.

He wailed for hours on end and I would sit by him with breasts literally bursting with milk. It was torture for us both. My body was physically aching to comfort him. I clearly remember standing by his crib and telling him that when we could start feeding I would never deny him. I said we would sleep side by side and he could feed whenever he wanted and for however long he wanted. I focused all of my energy into expressing so that when he was well enough he could receive my milk drop by drop via a feeding tube. I pumped every three hours for weeks—the hospital fridges were overflowing—I gave dairy farmers a run for their money.

Two excruciatingly long weeks later, I was finally allowed to feed my baby. I was told it may take a while for him to latch on, but before the nurse had finished her sentence he was on—suckling away like he'd been doing it every minute of the day. This was one of the best moments of my life. We recognised early on that breastfeeding was more than nourishment for us; it was an emotional connection. It was a bond; much-needed comfort between a mother and her son who had been through the most traumatic experience. It was something we would never take for granted.

Although he fed easily, our journey wasn't without its challenges. At about six weeks I developed nipple vasospasm, which meant that due to poor circulation and cold extremities, I would have intense, toe-curling pain every time I fed. I would be in tears coming up to feed time and even though it was summer, I had to wear socks and gloves when I fed. I was quite the sight—a topless, crying mad woman with a breast pump on one nipple and a baby on the other, wearing socks, gloves and undies. But I persevered and it subsided within a few weeks. Then we went through the teething/biting phase at eight to nine months, but this, too, passed and we continued to feed into his second year of life.

When my daughter was born, she was only 2.8 kilograms. There had been an issue with the placenta that wasn't picked up until after she was born. I thought that after feeding my son for so long I would be an expert the second time around. Wrong.

My nipples were like sandpaper. It was so painful I would cry leading up to feeds. Had I not had the feeding experience with my son, I probably would have given up. I knew it would get easier, so I persevered. She was so small and needed to feed all the time to catch up—I'm talking every one to two hours. Some suggested she wasn't getting enough milk and that I should 'top her up' with a bottle, but luckily I had learned it was all about supply and demand, and that it took up to six weeks to establish a good rhythm. She was gaining weight and length, and by six weeks, she had gone from the 5th to the 50th percentile on the growth chart.

I share this story because I truly feel like breastfeeding education is the most under-resourced area of early motherhood. I think most of us have experienced first-hand the conflicting and often outdated advice from well-meaning friends, family, midwives and doctors. Whenever I am asked for tips on breastfeeding, my first response is to book in with a qualified lactation consultant, preferably before the birth, and definitely after the birth, too. It is really important that you learn what to expect with breastfeeding and what is normal—and 'normal' can be different depending on your situation, birth experience, etc. It's your breastfeeding journey—it's a two-way relationship between both you and your baby, and you and your lactation consultant.

The education and knowledge around breastfeeding has changed so much since our mothers had us, so your mother and mother-in-law are not always the best people to take advice from. Similarly, GPs know a little about a lot of things, but they haven't had the specific training of a lactation consultant.

It's your breastfeeding journey—it's a two-way relationship between both you and your baby, and you and your lactation consultant.

So if you would like to breastfeed (it's important to note that it's a choice), ease up on the expectations. Don't put too much pressure on yourself. See a lactation consultant and learn what is normal, surround yourself with supportive people and take it one day at a time. Trust your gut, and your body. If you choose not to breastfeed, that's OK, too! But for those who want to try, you need to make sure you have adequate support throughout the process.

Because I like to practise what I preach, I have asked breastfeeding consultant and midwife Amberley Harris to share five top tips on breastfeeding. Before I hand it over to her, I need to state that this is only a guide. If you don't do all of these things, a healthy breastfeeding relationship is still possible for you. I was induced with an epidural in both of my pregnancies, and introduced a dummy to my babies, and both of them breastfed successfully. These tips are designed to give you the best possible chance. If you do these things and still can't manage to breastfeed—for whatever reason—don't beat yourself up. From an adult who was only breastfed for six weeks, I can assure you it's all OK.

A MODERN MAMA'S GUIDE
TO BREASTFEEDING

BY AMBERLEY HARRIS, BREASTFEEDING CONSULTANT AND MIDWIFE

Breastfeeding is the new black, there's no doubt about it, but it's important to point out that for many mamas, breastfeeding can be hard to establish. It's like any skill; it takes practise. The time it takes to establish breastfeeding is around six weeks. Six often long and possibly super-challenging weeks. But here's the good news: if you make it through this time, the odds are, *Hunger Games*-style, in your favour; and you are likely to go on and successfully breastfeed that little dreamboat of yours.

To increase your chances of successfully breastfeeding your baby, I have put together my top five breastfeeding tips for the modern mama.

1 ALLOW YOUR BABY TO CHOOSE ITS BIRTHDAY.

Ideally, aim to have a spontaneous, physiological birth, and avoid any drugs or medical interventions, as these can affect your baby's instinctive breast-seeking behaviours. Babies are born with a genetic blueprint for breastfeeding.

Do your research on all the various birthing interventions on breastfeeding (pain relief options, induction methods, caesareans, etc.,) so you know what to avoid, where possible, in order to give your baby the best chance to tap into this genetic blueprint.

2 ALLOW YOUR BABY TIME TO SELF-ATTACH AT THE FIRST BREASTFEED.

On average, it takes a baby 30 to 60 minutes to complete the 'breast crawl' (when a newborn instinctively moves towards the nipple and starts to feed on its own) and self-attach to the breast post-birth. So, if any doctors or midwives are giving your bubba the hurry up, politely ask for their patience so you can give your darling baby the vital time he or she deserves.

3 BREASTFEED ON DEMAND.

This means whenever your baby wants to feed, you feed them, which is roughly every two to three hours in the early days and weeks. This will help your boobs get the memo and bring in an

abundant milk supply; it also ensures your baby will be less likely to have significant weight loss in the first few days.

4 AVOID DUMMIES, BOTTLES AND FORMULA.
These may negatively affect your breastfeeding relationship with your baby by reducing your milk supply and the chances of your baby learning how to successfully breastfeed. NB: After six weeks, you are fine to introduce a dummy or a weekly bottle of expressed breast milk without these compromising your breastfeeding.

5 SEEK PROFESSIONAL SUPPORT.
Find someone you connect with and trust before your baby's birth and engage in some antenatal breastfeeding education with them. Have an appointment together, watch some educational videos they recommend, do some reading, etc. Then, promise yourself (and your babe) that you are going to devote the first six weeks of your little one's life to working with your chosen breastfeeding specialist in order to learn how to breastfeed. Research tells us if you have the right support and you make it to the golden six-week mark, you're more likely to shine at breastfeeding.

Breastfeeding for me was so much more than

nourishing my child.

It was a soul connection. A secret love language ...

FED IS BEST

However you feed your baby—by breast or by bottle—it should never be controversial. I find it ludicrous that we are still having this debate. Whether you bottle-feed a three-month-old or breastfeed a two-year old—we should be able to feed our babies without shame. In fact, we should be able to celebrate it.

When my daughter was four months old, I was approached by a global company to create content to feature on my Instagram page. They wanted to break the stigma of 'perfect' Instagram moments and show the real, raw side of motherhood. This is easy, I thought. My husband had been away for a couple of weeks; I was solo parenting while trying to work. I had both kids sleeping with me every night—I was exhausted and 'touched out'. I had zero personal space. So I submitted a selfie of me on my bed with my son's feet in my face and my daughter nursing. You could barely make out she was nursing—you definitely couldn't see any nipple, or even breast skin, as her head was covering it.

'Use breasts to sell everything from burgers to cars and no one bats an eye. Use breasts to feed babies as nature intended, and everyone loses their mind.'

— **THE WILD WOMAN SISTERHOOD**

They rejected the image because 'breastfeeding can be seen as controversial'. Controversial. To feed your own child, as nature intended, was controversial? I realised in that moment that we still had a long way to go when it came to society's perception of breastfeeding.

Back when I'd sat next to my sick newborn in the NICU and listened to him scream in hunger for weeks, I would have given anything to give him the breast or a bottle. So, instead of judging, let's take a moment to consider the parents of tube-fed babies, and realise how lucky we are to even have that choice.

When friends asked if I was 'still breastfeeding?' past one year, their response was rarely, 'Wow, good on you.' I was often met with shocked expressions and advice on how to be strict and say 'no'. I was actually told by a breastfeeding mother that I was either 'a freak or mad' for breastfeeding so long. I know my son didn't 'need' it for survival (I was told this continually by everyone, too) but he needed it for comfort. To me, his emotional need was just as important as the physical, nutritional need (of course, there are still nutritional benefits, too). And so I continued.

I gave up trying to defend my decision and in the last year I actually hid the fact that I still nursed from those who didn't know. I found support through online communities with like-minded mothers who helped me realise I wasn't alone, and that it was actually quite normal for some one- to two-year-olds to still be feeding through the night. I also connected with some mamas through Instagram—one in particular who had a boy the same age as my son. Like me, she felt ready to stop breastfeeding, but wanted her son to be ready enough so that weaning was a gentle, gradual process. I can't tell you what a difference it makes to connect with another mother who totally gets you. We sent each other 'Boob File' updates and have supported each other throughout weaning.

There is not one part of me that regrets nursing my son for two years. The only regret I have is that I let other people's judgements get to me. So with my daughter, I was more confident in my breastfeeding decisions.

I feel just as strongly about women being shamed for choosing not to or being unable to breastfeed. Most new mums want more than anything to have a beautiful breastfeeding relationship, but sometimes, despite their best efforts, it just doesn't work out—sometimes physically and sometimes emotionally. I have seen members of my own family struggle with the guilt of not being able to nurse their babies. We don't know the backstory of everyone's choices, but what we do know is that every mum is doing the best they can with their current circumstance.

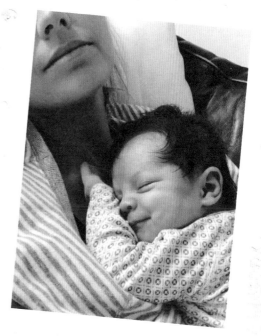

This comparison is what tears women and mothers apart. Our babies need happy, loving parents—not self-doubting, anxious mums that are scared to feed their screaming babies—a breast or bottle—for fear of judgement.

So my message to all mamas is to carry on! Feed with pride—covered, uncovered, private, public, breast or bottle. Just like everything in motherhood—we all do it differently, and that's OK!

DEAR 'JUDGY MUM'

BY MOTHER ANITA HEIGLAUER

Five years ago, I decided to undergo a preventative double mastectomy due to multiple breast cancer cases in my immediate family. This meant all of my breast tissue was removed and reconstructed by means of cosmetic surgery.

It was one of the hardest decisions I have ever had to make as it brought with it the possibility that I would never be able to breastfeed my children, should I ever be lucky enough to conceive. The recovery was long and painful, and as I found out only after having given birth to my beautiful daughter, it was not the end of the story.

Being a mum who gives her newborn baby a bottle turned me immediately into a selfish, uncaring and irresponsible mother. Or so I was made to believe.

People would approach me asking me whether I would be breastfeeding. Breastfeeding mothers would claim in my presence they would never give their child the bottle. Not to mention the judgemental glances of passers-by or acquaintances.

Some nurses in the hospital had no tolerance for me not even trying. They had me get up off my bed to get my daughter's formula myself, despite me having had emergency surgery the day before.

One might say that it should have just bounced off of me, as I knew the real reason behind why I could not breastfeed, but that was easier said than done. As a first-time mum, you're naturally insecure already, and being treated like that only makes it worse.

Now that my daughter has just celebrated her first birthday and I am settled into motherhood, I know that being a good mother has nothing to do with whether you have been able to breastfeed or not.

Yes, I would have given anything for that bond you can immediately create by giving your child this part of yourself. And yes, I still mourn for this feeling every once in a while.

But I realised that bonding can happen in other ways. I am lucky enough to raise my daughter bilingually, and as a self-employed mum, I can work around her schedule. This is my way of bonding—of creating this special connection that hopefully lays the groundwork for her to grow up to be an inspired young woman who will always speak for herself and stand her ground.

So I urge you, please don't judge a book by its cover. Either read a couple of pages or don't judge at all.

chapter six:
relationships.

A letter to you

Dear Mum,

I get it now. Everything you said, everything you did—it all makes sense. I used to think you never got sick. Now I know you did—you just didn't say anything. Do you know I still call for you when I'm sick or in pain? There are certain things only mums can make better.

You comforted me through heartbreaks. You hid my first concert outfit from Dad. You were at every recital, hat parade and school concert. You were always there cheering us on at the finish line or waiting at the ambulance when I got that epic stitch. You were always there. For decades, you drove us to netball and soccer and dancing. And somehow dinner was always on the table when we got home.

I just thought these were the things mums did. Now I understand this was just part of what you did. You were so much more. You are so much more.

You protected us from things we only learned after we became adults. Now I understand you had your whole life, too. You just prioritised ours.

Marcia xo

As soon as you have your baby, your relationships will change. And I mean every relationship. With your family, your friends and your partner.

My relationships with my mum and sister became stronger. I didn't expect this shared understanding—this bond of 'motherhood'— to be so strong. I have a whole new level of adoration for them both.

FIND YOUR TRIBE

Everyone warned me motherhood would be hard. It was and it still is, but not so much in the ways I had imagined it would be. The sleepless nights were exhausting—but I got through. The endless laundry was monotonous,

but not hard. What I did find difficult was going from a social work environment to pretty much zero adult conversation, day in and day out. It was isolating and lonely.

Those early days are so foreign and confusing. You really do need backup. A sounding board—preferably someone else who is going through the same stage to say, 'WTF is this?!' It takes a village, mamas, and you need to find yours. But as a twenty-something, thirty-something or forty-something woman, it can be a little daunting to make new friends— especially if you already have a friendship crew.

The good thing about meeting new mum friends is you don't really need any 'ice breaker' conversations. Let's just say there's nothing like discussing vaginal tears and haemorrhoids while simultaneously wiping a butt to fast-track a friendship.

I never went to an official 'mother's group'. My own mother (who admittedly is a bit of an introvert) described it as a 'competitive' environment. This isn't true for everyone, of course, but my son only came home from hospital at five to six weeks, so I felt like I missed the boat anyway. Thankfully one of my best friends had a baby a few months before I was due, so I met some other new mums through her. We called ourselves the 'renegade mother's group' and it made the first year so much more enjoyable. I went from back-to-back nappy changes broken up with laundry and a few rounds of singing 'Twinkle, Twinkle, Little Star', to play dates with rosé on a school day! These friendships and weekly catch-ups were truly my saving grace.

Mother's groups have their place but they can be a bit hit or miss, especially when the only thing you have in common is that you had a baby. You may just meet your mama-friend 'match', but if you don't, that's OK. This is where apps and social media come in.

It wasn't until I joined Instagram in my second year of motherhood that I truly felt like I found my tribe. I connected with so many like-minded mums. Our friendships began because we all had babies, but we connected through other shared interests— fashion, music, art—aspects of our 'pre-mum' selves. It was an undeniably supportive community when it began. We celebrated milestones and monotony—we didn't question each other's choices, we had each other's backs. Some lived nearby and some lived on the other side of the world, but these were my people. I spoke to them every day. That is the wonderful thing about online communities. For all of their failings, I have truly met some of my best friends online and have gone on to meet and adore many of them in 'real life'. Surround yourself with people who lift you up. These people make up your tribe.

A letter to my husband

FROM MOTHER.LY

Dear husband,

It won't always be like this. Our lives will not always feel like we are rushing, like we're perpetually late, like we're always playing catch-up.

Life won't always be this raising-little-kids level of chaos.

We won't always wake up exhausted because we've been woken up throughout the night. We won't always ask (beg) our kids to have three more mouthfuls of dinner while we scoff ours down. We won't always be too tired for date nights—to get dressed up, think of a place to go and actually go there together, by ourselves, to enjoy adult conversation.

We won't always feel so overwhelmed.

One day we will have children who are grown up and need us less.

Maybe then, we'll have more time to go out on more dates and more energy to engage in meaningful conversations before bed.

But, right now, we have all of this.

All of this beauty. All of this wonder. All of this joy.

I'm sure that someday we'll miss this madness. The morning snuggles when they no longer want to pile into bed with us. We'll miss the dance parties in the living room, the weekends at the park. Maybe we'll miss all of the noise and all of the mess.

We will miss this stage of our lives together. So, for now, let's try and laugh the frustrations off, and try and sneak in some kisses.

Let's be in this. Together.

Because before them, it was us. And after them, it'll be us.

And when they go off to write their own stories, I'll still be here. Ready to write the next chapter with you.

— ORIGINALLY PUBLISHED ON MOTHER.LY BY COLLEEN TEMPLE

PARTNER

When you have a child, the most significant relationship shift will be with your partner. Good, bad or just different—having a baby changes your relationship dynamics. All of a sudden it's about the baby. Everything else is put on the backburner.

My husband wanted babies before I did. As soon as we got married he had babies on the brain. I didn't feel that maternal drive, and to prove my point (and buy myself another year), I decided to cycle through Cambodia on a charity mission that required six months of training.

When I returned from my trip, I felt 'ready'. OK, that's a lie, I wasn't sure if I would ever feel truly 'ready' . . . until we were trying for a few months and it wasn't happening.

I grew up in a large family. There were eight years between my youngest siblings and I, and then my mother started fostering babies, so I had a fair idea of what motherhood entailed. I knew it wouldn't be all rainbows and lollipops; my husband, on the other hand, did not. So when our gorgeous little bundle arrived in all his reflux, no-sleep glory—life, as my husband knew it, was turned on its head. The daily 'witching hour' screaming sessions (before he was diagnosed with reflux) put so much pressure on us. And by witching hour I mean 'witching three to four hours'.

One of my earliest memories of us as a family of three is of sitting in our tiny apartment as my husband was swaddling, swaying and shushing a screaming baby in his arms, complaining, huffing and puffing in frustration. I screamed at him over the screaming baby, 'Well, what did you think it would be like?' 'NOT THIS!' was his response. Then I went into defence of said screaming baby and it started one of many, many strained relationship moments.

We often talk about post-partum depression and adjusting to a new life for the mother, but it's important to remember that a father is adjusting to his new role, too.

I have been with my husband for fourteen years. I remember the first time I saw him: my heart skipped a beat as if it knew it had found its mate. We stayed up talking all night and he told me we would get married. I told him that was very presumptuous, but here we are, fourteen years together and almost ten married. We are deep in the tag-teaming trenches of early parenthood. It's been the most trying stage of our relationship. But we're doing the damn thing together.

We've navigated fertility, loss and IVF together. He was holding my hand when we lost our babies and he was holding my hand when I birthed our babies.

We've been through the highest of highs and the lowest of lows, together. We've had huge achievements and miserable fails, together. For years, I stood by his side and held the fort as he travelled for work to create his dream. I remember counting my son's 'baths' until he got home. 'Nineteen baths to go . . .' Now he is holding the fort and helping me bring my dreams to life.

It's not easy. Some days we wish we had more babies; other days we want a break. We argue a lot. We're stressed and tired and prioritise everything else over our relationship. I don't remember the last time we had a date or discussed anything other than work or kids. But I know we are in this together. That we still laugh, together. Because as in that letter, before them, it was just us. And after them, it will be us.

Parenting is a team sport. Not a competition. It's not a score sheet of who showered last, slept the most and looked after the kids last. This reminder is for me as much as anyone else—it's easy to fall back into this dynamic. We have been there time and again, and it's not a healthy place.

One of the best pieces of wisdom I received was this: if you don't want your husband or partner to think of themselves as a 'babysitter' or 'part-time carer', then don't treat them that way. The first time around, I was so convinced that only I could feed, bath or change the baby the 'right' way. My poor husband didn't know what to do or how to help. All I wanted was help, but of course he never did things the 'right' way. The second time around, I was more relaxed; we discussed the specific responsibilities he was in charge of—like bathing the baby. And if he didn't know what he was doing, then I would let him figure things out for himself.

Understanding and respecting each other's responsibilities as parents is so crucial to your relationship with one another. There's a funny meme floating around that says, 'He asked why the house isn't clean since I'm home all day. I asked why we aren't rich since he works all day.' Regardless of whether you're at home all day taking care of the baby or you're at work trying your hardest to make financial ends meet, you're doing the best that you can for your family.

DATE YOUR *PARTNER*

BY FREELANCE WRITER AND EDITOR JESSICA BOSCO

Finding time for romance among the chaos of kids and family life can seem near impossible.

With our lives feeling like they're just getting busier and busier, there are so many other priorities that continue to get in the way. The endless to-do lists, demanding little ones and that little thing called sleep deprivation all make the thought of dressing up and heading out for a date night and a little romance fall into the too-hard basket.

And while we know that when it comes to parenting you can't pour from an empty cup (well, we know this, but we don't always practise what we preach, do we?), the same goes for relationships. Just like you've got to prioritise self-care, you've also got to nurture your relationship.

When it seems like you are ships passing in the night, taking the time to share a cheeky pash in the pantry while the kids are watching *Peppa Pig*, sharing a bottle of wine and some takeaway once the kids go down or actually locking in a babysitter for a long overdue night out sans kids can work wonders for your relationship. Your kids will feed off this positive energy, too.

It doesn't have to be big grand gestures all the time (although those are great, too), but making the time to acknowledge each other, checking in and chatting about something other than the kids and heck, even getting a little freaky between the sheets, is so important.

Here are a few ideas to help you find time for each other among the madness of parenthood.

KEEP IT CHEAP AND CHEERFUL

Don't let date night be a source of financial stress—we all have enough of that already. Keep it simple with takeaway, going out to your favourite local haunt or cooking a meal at home once the kids go down.

GIFT IT

When it comes to Christmas or birthdays or even 'just because', give each other gifts that require getting out of the house, e.g. tickets to see a favourite band or a show. This way, there's plenty of time to book in a babysitter, and no room for excuses!

LOCK THEM IN, IN ADVANCE

Speaking of no excuses, locking in your date nights in advance and putting them in the calendar can help you work them into your schedule, rather than just trying to squeeze them in. Sure, this isn't as sexy and spontaneous as date night used to be, but you'll get back to that again one day!

DO A BABYSITTING SWAP

Good babysitters can be hard to come by, and trusting your precious little ones with a stranger can be a hard ask, so why not do a swap with some friends who are in the same boat as you? You could watch their kids one night while they go out, and then they could watch yours when you go out. This also saves money on paying for a sitter—double win!

DATE NIGHT AT HOME

Sometimes getting out of the house can just be impossible—especially when you have a newborn! So take the time to connect with each other at home. Plan a dinner and enjoy a bottle of wine once the kids go to sleep.

DAY DATES

If you just can't find the time for a night out, then what about during the day? Enjoy a little romance in the light of day when the kids are in day care or at school, or drop them off with friends or family. Head out for a nice lunch in the sunshine, or to the beach or have a picnic in the park.

NETFLIX AND CHILL

Get hooked on a series together and cosy up on the couch. Not all intimacy has to be in the bedroom—there's nothing like having a good old snuggle on the couch. It's up to you where you go with the 'chill' . . .

TURN OFF THE TV

That said, make sure you take the time to turn off the TV and spend time together and connect. Play a board game, talk, take a bath or even give each other massages!

DATING BUCKET LIST

Create a dating bucket list that contains all the things you want to do and places you want to go. But put a time limit on it and see how many you can tick off.

TAKE TURNS PLANNING SURPRISES

Again, these don't have to be big, grand gestures, but just take turns planning the dates and surprise your partner; it's the little things that count.

There's no denying that time is one of our most precious commodities, so if you feel like you just don't have enough of it, take stock of what is taking up your time. Are you or the kids taking on too many commitments? Are you catching up with people that don't bring out the best in you? Life is too short and too precious, so make time for the things that matter most to you.

FIRST COMES BABY
THEN COMES MARRIAGE

BY KELLY MÜLLER, FOUNDER OF KELLY MÜLLER CONSULTING

Whether it's by choice or circumstance, motherhood looks different on each of us. Just because you are a mum, it doesn't mean you are married to a man and have a white picket fence. There are de facto parents, divorced parents, single parents, same-sex parents, foster and adoptive parents, and they are all doing the best they can to raise these tiny humans. Here, we share—and celebrate—some wonderful women who sit outside of these parenting relationship 'norms'. — MARCIA

Conceiving out of wedlock was once discussed only in whispers and solved with a shotgun wedding, often followed with the surprise 'early' arrival of a baby. These days, the baby carriage often comes before marriage and it's really no big deal. Because committing to the endless demands of a baby is about as all-in as you're ever going to get.

My (now) husband Josh and I were together for five years before he proposed. He woke up one Sunday morning and asked me to marry him. It was simple, unexpected and understated. It was perfect. We decided we'd already waited long enough, so we started planning for the wedding in just four months' time. However, two months after the proposal, we found out we were having our first baby and our immediate wedding plans went out the window. Our darling daughter was born in September 2015, and we set our wedding date for six months later, back home in New Zealand.

Friends asked me whether I thought it was a good idea—we'd be sleep deprived, I might still be breastfeeding, how would we manage the day around her sleeps? Josh and I try to be fairly relaxed when it comes to the ebbs and flows of parenting, so we figured it would be what it would be. Getting married was important to us. It was about creating a family. It was a considered commitment to one another, and to Sunny, our daughter. And it was one of the most memorable days of our lives. Here are my tips for getting married with a bub in tow.

DO WHAT WORKS BEST FOR YOU.

People will tell you to 'get a good sleep the night before', however, emotions and excitement will be sure to keep you awake. Add a baby to the mix and 'a good night's sleep' is probably quite unlikely. I considered expressing and leaving Sunny with her grandmother, but given she was only six months old, exclusively breastfed and had never spent a night without me, it wasn't the time to try something new. Sunny stayed with me the night before and shared my bed. Co-sleeping for us meant fewer distractions and a faster turnaround time for feeds, which resulted in my version of a good night's sleep! Plus, it was super special to snug up with my daughter the night before I was to become a Mrs!

STICK TO YOUR REGULAR RHYTHM.

Weddings are overwhelming. In the lead up, the days are long and the excitement levels are high. We found sticking as close to our regular rhythm as we could worked well for us. I moved my hair and makeup to mid-morning and started our day just as we would have if we were at home. I strapped Sunny into the front pack, we went for a walk and I got my daily coffee.

TIME THE DAY AROUND SLEEPS.

You know your baby best, so when planning your day, consider their ideal sleep times and work backwards from there (though remember, it's not the end of the world if it doesn't work out exactly as you'd planned!). We set our ceremony for 3 p.m. knowing this was likely to be post-sleep and Sunny would be well rested. Worst-case scenario, our drive to the wedding was 30 minutes so I knew she'd at least get a catnap.

HAVE A GROUP TO HELP WITH BUB.

There will undoubtedly be a lot of friends and family eager for a cuddle with bub. Given we live in a different country to a lot of our family and friends, this is even more the case for us. Make it clear who is responsible for your baby so you have someone who recognises when she/he needs a little time out if you're not available. Post-ceremony was the most overwhelming part for Sunny, so I suggest having someone to take bub away every twenty minutes or so to let them regroup. As the bride and groom, we had to fit in multiple conversations with guests, family photos and toasts in this time, and Sunny was passed between a fair few people. She handled it really well but Josh and I were conscious that she needed some time out. My sister and I took her away from the crowd and let her kick around and play with her toys in the quiet for a while.

CONSIDER YOUR WEDDING STYLE.

Because we live in Australia and don't get to spend a lot of time with our friends and family in New Zealand, we went with an informal seating plan. We had a Mexican food truck in lieu of a sit-down dinner and the reception was set up with trestle tables, bar leaners and lounge suites. This worked for our guests and for our baby because there were different areas that she could kick back in, without being confined to a set place or arrangement. Depending on how long your bub will be part of the action, this is really important to consider.

JUST GO WITH IT.

While we had a run sheet with preferred timings, we were open to moving things around if needed. When it came to the speeches, we pushed them out a bit while we settled Sunny for another nap. We had the first speeches while she slept and managed to fit in a dance, drink and some food together, then Josh and I hit the floor for our speeches once she woke up.

After the speeches, it was party time! But it was clear that Sunny was starting to get tired and it was getting a bit much. I headed up to the house and fed her before handing her over to my mother-in-law to put her to bed. It had been a long day for our baby and she was a little unsettled. Our grand plans of getting her to bed then enjoying the wedding together until home time didn't quite work out—she gave Grammy a little bit of grief and wouldn't properly settle with anyone other than Josh or myself. Between the three of us, we took turns rocking her into a sweet slumber, and then Grammy stayed up at the house with her.

While it meant we spent a bit of time away from our guests, I felt so incredibly happy and fulfilled walking back down to the dance floor and seeing everyone having such a great time. Weddings are about friends, family, great music, great food and a whole lot of love—and ours was certainly that! Don't put too much pressure on yourself to do everything exactly as you had planned or expected. Babies can be unpredictable, and just going with it keeps everyone a lot calmer!

CREATE A SENSE OF FAMILIARITY.

As our wedding was not only in unfamiliar territory but also a different country, I made sure I had a few things to remind Sunny of home. We had certain toys, blankets and her favourite pyjamas, and I also had my signature Ecoya candles burning throughout the day. I have Vanilla Bean candles in every room of our house, so I had these on the tables at the wedding as well.

SEE THE GOOD IN EVERY SITUATION.

In what I am sure will be a tale to tell in years to come, we spent our wedding night at Josh's parents' house, with our baby girl snugged up between us. We hired a house for our bridal party and ourselves but as they all got quite drunk and rowdy—and Sunny had had a huge day—we decided to take her home where it was quiet. It is a super-special memory in hindsight; we woke up together as a family!

SINGLE MUM *DIARIES*

BY LEILA STEAD, BLOGGER AND FOUNDER OF THE SINGLE MUM DIARIES

I became a single mother-to-be in December 2015 at just thirteen weeks' pregnant with my now three-year-old daughter, Ever. I came from a single-parent household and although I never aspired to be a mother, I knew that if motherhood was something I was destined to do, I would want to do it in love and in a family—that I would create my own family and it would be the type of family I never had as a child: together, loving, supportive and stable.

I never got that family. I became a single mother the moment my partner left and the pressure to somehow create that family I had dreamed of was entirely on my shoulders. It has been three years since he left us, and what I can tell you now is that we are whole, we are together, we are loving, we are supportive and we are stable. Just the two of us. The ending to a relationship doesn't define who you are, but the way in which you define yourself after the loss of a relationship can determine how quickly you rise and take hold of the reins again.

Now, I am creating a life more beautiful than the traditional family life I had dreamed of as a child. I want you to know that if I can do it, you can, too.

I was left while pregnant. I had just lost my job, I didn't have any savings and I had bills that my partner had left me with. I barely had any furniture, and what little I did have I had to put into storage so I could move back in with my family at age twenty-nine and pregnant with my first child. That was my rock bottom and it hurt like hell. But if I can rebuild my life, piece by piece, dollar by dollar, day by day from the ground up, then I promise that you can too.

Since entering motherhood, my favourite quote has been the well-known adage, 'this, too, shall pass'. It does, it always does, and it's up to you to decide how you want to walk through it. In motherhood, we need to find our tribe and yes, as the saying goes, we need to love our children hard. They will become your rock. When you get lost among all the routines and the mundane tasks that come with motherhood, they will remind you how to love yourself again. They will remind you of the mother you are, of the woman you are underneath it all, and that we all stand in this together. If you find yourself knee-deep in motherhood, lost somewhere among a washing pile and dry shampoo, remind yourself that this, too, shall pass.

RAINBOW *FAMILY*

BY KEREN MORAN, THE CO-FOUNDER OF MEMEME PRESS

Noa and I had been together for sixteen years before our daughter, Neko, was born. We went from being a 'gay couple' to being a 'rainbow family'.

Apart from the standard, absolutely life-altering experiences of becoming parents, we were also very aware of having brought a new little person into a world that hadn't entirely made up its mind as to whether it was OK for us to even be a family.

We knew that part of our new job would be framing her world in terms that made her feel loved and safe, and ultimately just as worthy as the next person.

Don't get me wrong—we're very lucky. Neko is very lucky. We live in Sydney and she is growing up in a time and a place where the make up of her family is just one thread in a rich tapestry of diverse families around us. We are not alone, and you don't need to be gay to have a 'different' family. And by 'different' I mean only that it departs from some elusive normative structure.

Neko's daycare, for example, was a heady mix of gay, single, divorced, blended extended and yes 'normal' families, all meshed together in a happy, hectic mishmash of culture and community.

A perfect backdrop for the kids to conduct guided explorations of what family means, what their place in the family means and how their family is the same and also different to other families. The kids—our kid included—were obsessed with this.

At home we talked and sang and read, flipping through picture books about everything from unicorns and mushrooms to sparrows in rice bags in India. What we couldn't seem to find enough books about, however, were families like ours.

Kids make sense of their world through the books they are read and the books they read. At the risk of sounding melodramatic, we felt we owed it to our kid to change what we could.

But we didn't want it to be just about our family. All families are different and we wanted to create a book that would let any kid be the star. We wanted it to be customisable, so that they are the centre of their story, with their very own family wrapped lovingly around them.

We wanted to make a book that promotes literacy and a love of reading through storytelling and beautiful illustrations. This is how Mememe Press was born.

LET'S TALK ABOUT **SEX, BABY**

BY PSYCHOLOGIST DANIELLE MALONEY

After having a baby there are so many factors that influence intimacy with your partner. Let's be honest, for a little while there—or maybe a long while—you probably won't want anything touching you. Anywhere. Well at least I didn't. On the physical side, I was recovering from an episiotomy and stitches as well as mentally still processing the trauma and memory of pushing out a watermelon-sized baby. Then there is the emotional side of simply being exhausted; being all-consumed with your baby, not feeling attractive, getting used to your new body and, if you're breastfeeding, feeling 'touched out'. So again, I have called in an expert to help guide us through the new normal of sex after baby. — MARCIA

Post-partum sex can be one hell of a roller coaster. I mean, between the nappies, sleep deprivation, constipation, breastfeeding, mood swings, aching boobs . . . the desire for sex has completely dried up, among other things (pun intended). When you make the first attempt—hell, it makes losing your virginity feel like a breeze. It can be painful, really painful. And awkward, really awkward. Many women report that it is almost like having to start over.

For many couples, the more babies you have, the less sex you have. I see so many people who say they really love sex while pregnant and after. Yeah, not me. I couldn't imagine anything worse than sex when heavily pregnant. Or even when I wasn't huge with a baby, I just felt like vomiting or sleeping. My libido was about as existent as a unicorn. In fact, my husband would have had more chance of catching a unicorn than having sex with me when pregnant. #sorrybabe

So here are a couple of tips of the trade to get the ball rolling . . .

PUT THE BRAKES ON, SISTER

There is no need to rush jumping back in the sack. It is really important that you give yourself time to heal, both physically and emotionally. We get so caught up in being the best mum and wife that we seem to forget about ourselves in the process. We neglect the intensity of labour and what our bodies go through, and how hard the adjustment is of bringing a child into the home. Besides, experts say that allowing your body adequate time to heal limits the amount of pain you feel when you start having sex again. So, don't rush this process; you have to put your own oxygen mask on before you can assist anyone else.

TALK IT OUT

By nature, we rely on assumptions to make sense of our reality, so it is easy for either you or your partner to make knee-jerk assumptions about the lack of sex in your relationship post-partum. Things like, 'they don't find me attractive anymore' or 'watching the birth has traumatised him and he doesn't find me sexually attractive anymore' are all familiar tunes. Talk to your partner, let them know how you're feeling and reassure them that it is not personal.

DON'T AIM FOR A HOME RUN

Sex is so much more than just intercourse. Use this post-partum time to explore first, second and third base. Reconnect and explore each other without penetration.

Spice up your erotic repertoire; play, caress, massage, fondle, explore, kiss, talk . . . you get the drill. To boot, novelty stimulates the release of dopamine, which in turn stimulates the pleasure centres in your brain, so this kind of intimacy can feel even more pleasurable than good ole missionary.

PUT IT IN THE DIARY

Welcome to the era of the most planned and organised sex you could ever have. It's not all bad and it does not mean spontaneity is lost, but the urge to jump your partner's bones is often outweighed by any one of your new little one's needs. And this only becomes more exaggerated as they get older. So plan it, make time for it; suck up to the in-laws to babysit one night. That way, you and your partner can go slow, take your time and enjoy it. After all, this is about pleasure, right?

PREPARE FOR ACTION

When D-Day arrives, come prepared with lubricant. Post-partum vaginal dryness is common and is caused by lower levels of oestrogen. It is more marked in women who breastfeed, as their levels of oestrogen are even more depleted because prolactin—the hormone that maintains milk production—is released. This is no way indicative of your level of sexual desire for your partner or their capacity to arouse you. It's just your body doing its thing.

Also, it is worth mentioning that organising contraception is a good idea.

There is a myth that breastfeeding can delay fertility, and to some extent it does. However, often a woman will ovulate before the return of her period, therefore you might miss the markers and run the risk of falling pregnant. Do your due diligence for your own peace of mind.

REMEMBER, THIS WILL PASS

Our minds are the world's greatest storytellers. Before we know it, our minds have scripted an ending that is not only inaccurate, but also discouraging and distressing about our post-partum sex life. Of course, post-partum sex is not without its challenges, but the road to recovery is time-limited. Be kind to yourself, have patience and focus on the here and now. And be mindful of those wretched thoughts that lead you astray.

So, what are you waiting for? Get your in-laws on the phone and organise that night in. A long, uninterrupted shower, your favourite movie, home-delivered pizza and some heavy petting may be just what you need.

While sex offers a way for you to connect and build intimacy with your partner, there are other ways to meet your significant other's desires. Ramblin Mama tweeted the hilarious words on the opposite page a few years ago. They sum up a feeling most mothers have experienced at some point along the journey about catering to their partners' needs. — MARCIA

Me:

Do that thing I like.

Husband:

(takes the kids & leaves)

— RAMBLIN MAMA VIA TWITTER

chapter seven: parenting.

So we've navigated the pregnancy, the birth and the bubble—now the real fun begins! Laura from parenting blog Chaos & Quiet tweeted a few years ago, 'Parenting is 50 per cent feeling like your head might explode, and 50 per cent feeling like your heart might.' Parenting is just as hard as it is beautiful.

Nothing in your lifetime will have such a profound effect on you in every way. You will never know a love like it—without condition, without wanting something in return. It really is the most precious gift.

There will also be nothing in your lifetime that will challenge you in so many ways. And those challenges change and evolve as your child grows.

You can adore your children, and still admit it is hard. You can be eternally grateful, and still be over it at times. Parenting is a wild ride, that's for sure.

SO HOW DO WE DO IT?

Well, that's the thing—I don't think any of us really know what we're doing. We're all just winging it. I thought the 'mummy-ness' would kick in for me eventually, but some days, even though I'm eight years in, I still feel like an imposter! I wonder if our mums ever felt the same?

The famous saying by author Jill Churchill, 'There's no way to be a perfect mother and a million ways to be a good one,' has become my parenting mantra. I think it really sums up modern parenting. The old school 'Do as

I say, not as I do' mentality just doesn't fly with a lot of parents anymore; many are choosing to teach through example rather than rules. The end game is to raise kind, resilient, respectful and confident humans, but there are so many ways to get there. The most important thing is that you are on the same page as your partner. Easier said than done, right?

I never thought I would be a co-sleeping, extended-breastfeeding mama, but here I am. I've had zero personal space since 2011, but you know what? I love it. My sister is a 'routine' mum—and that works for her. I don't think we really know what our parenting style will be until after we have a baby, and I think most of us can identify with elements from a few different styles. Every baby and every situation is different. Just do what works for you.

Best parenting advice
I have for new parents:

There is no advice.

It's hard. It's amazing.

Everyone around you will have a different opinion on everything.

I hope you like to pee with an audience.

Good Luck.

— SCARY MOMMY VIA TWITTER

DON'T SEE THE LABEL . . .

EARTH
MUM

FIT
MUM

GLAM
MUM

HOT MESS
MUM

WINE
MUM

CAREER
MUM

HELICOPTER
MUM

INSTA
MUM

SEE THE PERSON

Breastfeeds into toddlerhood because stopping was more effort than continuing.

Says no to sugar in coffee, but polishes off a block of chocolate at 10 p.m.

Exercises once a week, but is in activewear on at least two more occasions.

Used to manage teams of people and million-dollar budgets, now loses negotiations with a tiny dictator who refuses to have their nappy changed.

Adds a red lip and heels, but hasn't showered in two days.

Counts down until bedtime, only to gaze lovingly at photos of their baby once they are asleep.

Uses non-toxic beauty products, but is not averse to some injectables.

Works 184 23-minute shifts a week, mostly after 10 p.m.

May not have gotten out of her pyjamas or cooked dinner, but closed a $10k deal on her phone.

Will bribe with chocolate (usually fair-trade, dairy-free, orangutan friendly).

YES, YOU CAN BE GRATEFUL AND OVER IT

I remember waking up one Sunday and for the first time in seven years of parenting I said to my husband, 'I don't want to parent today.' I really didn't. I just wanted a day off. I was sick, the kids were sick. My daughter was simultaneously teething and in some kind of 'wonder week'; my son had to go to a birthday party where I would have to make small talk with other adults. I'd overcommitted with work. I was tired. I hadn't slept a full night in a year. I was just craving a day to myself. A day without being poked, prodded, pulled at, whined at . . . without being touched. But as soon as those words were out of my mouth, I felt a huge rush of guilt.

I am beyond grateful for my kids—they are my biggest blessings and I rarely complain (out loud) because I have the perspective to know how lucky I am. They are my world. My life. I tell them I love them a billion times a day. I show them I do . . . but I am still tired. I still lose my shit a few too many times. I still hide in the pantry and eat Nutella from the jar. One of my light-bulb parenting moments was the realisation that you can be grateful, but still be over it. That sometimes it's OK to say f*#k this, let's start again tomorrow.

Being a parent is all-consuming. There are so many conflicting emotions. It's messy, challenging and exhausting, but still somehow the best thing ever. So if you're having one of 'those' days, just know you're not alone. I am forever grateful to be a mother, but a bit of personal space every now and then would be nice.

LET GO OF ANY JUDGEMENT

For any self-doubting, sleep-deprived, cracked-nippled new mum, the last thing you need is unsolicited advice on what you 'should' and 'shouldn't' be doing. There's a meme that says, 'Breastfed, bottle-fed, stay at home or work, we've all knocked our kid's head on the car trying to get them in the car seat.' The struggle is real and we don't need to be judged for trying to do our best.

It all begins as soon as that little embryo attaches to the uterine wall. People will tell you what to eat, what not to eat, how you should be carrying, if you are big, if you are little, that you must accrue sleep . . . some may even throw in a horror birth story for good measure.

Once you have the baby, it gets worse. Even though it's usually well-meaning, the amount of conflicting information you receive as a new parent can be overwhelming, to say the least. From midwives and mothers' groups to family members and friends, the 'shoulds' and 'shouldn'ts' come thick and fast and can lead to self-doubt—especially for an emotional new mum.

Advice is great when it's asked for, and sometimes even when it's not—as long as we are then confident enough to take the bits that fit with us and leave the rest. It's all about finding the way that works for us without the worry or fear of judgement for doing things differently.

This was one of the driving forces for me to start Not So Mumsy. I wanted to create a judgement-free space for new mums. As a new mother, I was expecting comments from older family members and midwives, but I wasn't prepared for the judgement from my peers—other new mums—especially when it came to feeding and sleeping. And in the early days, everything is about feeding and sleeping.

Advice is great when it's asked for, and sometimes even when it's not—as long as we are then confident enough to take the bits that fit with us and leave the rest. It's all about finding the way that works for us without the worry or fear of judgement for doing things differently.

Our catch-ups and conversations left me with so much self-doubt that I sought internet chat groups to check that my eight-month-old who fed on demand and woke throughout the night was normal. Turns out he was. After twelve months I was the only one in my mum circle that 'still' breastfed. The comments—even when they weren't direct—made me feel ashamed to feed him in public. I would never make a comment about a mum choosing to bottle-feed—for whatever reason—and I just expected the same in return. I felt so ashamed to be feeding my one-year-old that I once took him to a smelly toilet cubicle at a Yo Gabba Gabba! concert to feed him. When I came out, I promised myself I would never do that again.

Ironically it was the online community and social media—the land of the 'troll'—where I found the most support. Instagram can be a pretty negative and judgy place, but I found so much support by connecting with women from around the world.

I wish I'd read those words posted by Natural Mama Co. on the next page when I was in hospital with my son. They would have changed my experience as a first-time mother. I constantly felt I was doing something wrong by responding to my baby in the way that felt right for our family. A nurse told me I had to let my one-week-old baby who had just had surgery 'self soothe'. When we were establishing feeds a couple of weeks later, I was told I could feed him but I had to put him straight back. I wasn't allowed to hold or cuddle him. When the nurse saw how upset I was, she asked condescendingly, 'First-time parents?' What we need to remember is that we all have our own journey, our own choices and our own plan. That's what makes parenthood so special.

POST BY @naturalmamaco

'Imagine how much easier mum life would be if we were all told it's OK to hold your baby for as long as you want. It's OK to feed them to sleep; it's OK [for them] to sleep in the same room as you. It's OK to kiss them every minute of every day; it's OK for them to be clingy. It's OK for them to need you. It's OK for you to need them.'

By the time your child is in school, there is a whole new set of challenges. Whether you had a natural birth, breastfed, co-slept, or whether you potty trained early or when your toddler gave up the dummy will not matter. Nobody will care about any of these things. All that matters is that your child was loved. Is loved. No one has their child's best interest at heart more than a parent. We don't have to agree with one another, but we can still support each other.

TWEET FROM MyQuestionableLife/@2questionable

'Of course you judge parents in restaurants before you have kids. That's how the human race survives, each person thinking they can do it better before finding out no you fucking can't.'

RUBBISH THINGS
OTHER PARENTS SAY

BY SUSIE VERRILL, BLOGGER AND FOUNDER OF MILO & ME

OTHER PARENT: 'Are you STILL nursing?'
ME: No, I'm not STILL nursing. I'm nursing.

OTHER PARENT: 'You're making a rod for your own back with that one!'
ME: Because we didn't leave him to cry? Once, when my baby was about 10 days old, he cried every single time we put him down anywhere. I thought I'd put him in his swing and see how long it took him to calm himself down. Thirty-five minutes later, I was deaf, Milo [my son] was the colour of fire engines and I realised I wasn't cut out for not comforting the human I'd created.

OTHER PARENT: 'Oh, we were really strict about that.'
ME: This is always said when we mention that we co-sleep. Like it wasn't a well-thought-out, adult decision to share our bed and instead, from the offset, Greg and I just couldn't be arsed to move our baby into a cot.

OTHER PARENT: 'Wait until he's . . .'
ME: Three, running, climbing, going to school, a teenager, etc. There's no end to this one. If there's one thing I've learned, it's that there are good and bad points in each and every stage, so when someone tells you to wait with bated breath for the next diabolical experience you're about to have, ignore 'em. You've got through it so far.

OTHER PARENT: 'I'm sticking to feeding schedules.'
ME: If the baby seems hungry, they're probably hungry. Or they're one of the youngest pranksters ever. I used to hate being asked if I was 'stretching' my baby's food breaks out for a certain amount of hours, because he never bloody managed it, and then I'd feel stressed. It's not worth getting eggy over.

OTHER PARENT: 'Oh, it's OK. It'll just help his/her immune system.'
ME: This comment is often made whenever they're playing in dirt, rolling on the floor or being snogged by our dogs. I love it when

kids are free to get messy and run around like wild things outdoors, but I draw the line at our dogs tonguing my son's face . . . Mud? Yes. Canine germs? No.

OTHER PARENT: 'He's 42-months-old.'
ME: Stop it. Count in years now, your child is old enough to not look like a cute Winston Churchill.

OTHER PARENT: 'You can absolutely have it all.'
ME: You can, but one of the things you're trying to juggle probably won't be done to a great standard. Take my life, for example; if I'm firing on all cylinders work/parenting wise, then my house looks like a landfill site or I haven't texted four of my friends back.

PERSPECTIVE: FINDING JOY IN THE IN-BETWEEN

There is an old La Leche League breastfeeding story of two new mothers. One of them says with a tired voice, 'It's been way worse than I expected! If I'm not holding or nursing him, he's crying.' The other says, 'It's been much easier than I expected! All I have to do is hold him and nurse him and he is happy and calm.' Sometimes it just takes a change in mindset. Instead of saying, 'I have to . . .' maybe try, 'I get to . . .' Even on the toughest days, sometimes stepping back and looking at the bigger picture is just what we need to get us through.

I had a waking-every-40-minutes severe reflux baby who would only sleep on my chest for the first four months, but after everything we had been through, I was just grateful he was alive. Grateful I had a baby that woke up every 40 minutes. Had I not had that experience with my son, I am sure I would not have coped in those first few months. My miscarriages, my secondary fertility struggles and the loss of my sisters—all of these things have shaped my perspective and made me grateful for what I have. It doesn't mean I don't curse and have meltdowns, but at the end of every day I appreciate just how lucky I am to have a happy, healthy family.

I know some days are really hard, but I try not to wish them away. I try to find the magic in the mundane and the joy in the in-between because one day we will miss the chaos and those long, groundhog days. Our children will grow up and go on to live their own lives with their own families, and we will realise these were the days.

The poem overleaf, *The Last Time*, often does the rounds on social media, but no one knows who the author is. It's one that always stays with me. It's such a beautiful reminder to live in the now. It provides the ultimate perspective for every parent. I dare you not to cry.

The Last Time

AUTHOR UNKNOWN

From the moment you hold your baby in your arms,
You will never be the same.
You might long for the person you were before,
When you had freedom and time,
And nothing in particular to worry about.
You will know tiredness like you never knew it before,
And days will run into days that are exactly the same,
Full of feeding and burping,
Whining and fighting,
Naps, or lack of naps.
It might seem like a never-ending cycle.

But don't forget . . .
There is a last time for everything.

There will come a time when you will feed
Your baby for the very last time.
They will fall asleep on you after a long day
And it will be the last time you ever hold your sleeping child.

One day you will carry them on your hip then set them down,
And never pick them up that way again.
You will scrub their hair in the bath one night
And from that day on they will want to bathe alone.

They will hold your hand to cross the road,
Then never reach for it again.
They will creep into your room at midnight for cuddles,
And it will be the last night you ever wake to this.

One afternoon you will sing the 'Wheels on the Bus'
And do all the actions,
Then never sing them that song again.
They will kiss you goodbye at the school gate,
The next day they will ask to walk to the gate alone.
You will read a final bedtime story and wipe your last
Dirty face.
They will run to you with arms raised for the very
Last time.

The thing is, you won't even know it's the last time
Until there are no more times.
And even then, it will take you a while to realise.

So while you are living in these times,
Yemember there are only so many of them
Snd when they are gone, you will yearn for just one more day
Of them.
For one last time.

chapter eight: self-care.

For eight years I have been either trying
to conceive, pregnant or breastfeeding.
In that time I have had four pregnancies,
two babies, gone through IVF and breastfed
for a total of four years. That's eight years
of growing, nurturing and sustaining life.
Eight years of considering everything I
put in and on my body. At times it felt like
a sacrifice, but for the most part, it was an
absolute privilege to witness first-hand the
wonder of the female body. Towards the
end of breastfeeding my second child,
I started to feel like I needed some time
and space. Time for me—not the mama-me,
but me-me—to fill up my own cup with
what makes me happy.

We all know the importance of self-care. We hear about it all the time, but when you are juggling as much as you are in motherhood, it can be hard to put yourself first.

The good news is it doesn't have to be much. Self-care to you could mean a five-minute face care ritual, a yoga class, a blow-dry, blasting the radio in the car and singing to your favourite song or a hot chocolate at a cafe on your own.

Self-care is not just important for ourselves, but for our children, too. Yes, to be a happier mother, but also to teach our kids about self-love. Our children are sponges; they hear the way we talk to others and ourselves. I want my kids to see me prioritise self-care by doing things that make me feel good, both mind and body.

10 EASY WAYS TO SHOW YOURSELF SOME LOVE

1. Make that appointment (or do what you've been putting off).
2. Unfollow people on social media that don't make you feel good.
3. Praise yourself the way you praise your kids.
4. Quit the guilt.
5. Say 'no' to something and be OK with it.
6. Accept help and ask for it if you need it (even if that means getting a babysitter).
7. Exercise. It's just as much for mental health as it is for physical health. Find something you look forward to. Whether it's running, Pilates, rock climbing or tennis doesn't matter—just find some form of movement you enjoy.
8. Wear something that makes you feel amazing (even if you are overdressed).
9. Eat for nutrients and nourishment, but also for joy. Twenty per cent of food should be for the soul—always.
10. Make time for your friends—even if it's just a ten-minute phone catch-up. You'll never regret it.

We lose ourselves a
little when we become mothers.
But that's OK.
Mothers are awesome
at finding lost things.

— MUMLYFE

WHAT DOES A 'REAL MUM' LOOK LIKE?

It seems like we have a bit of a fixation on what a 'real' mum looks like. I often see comments on social media that say someone is or isn't a 'real' mum. Just to be clear, I want to point out that if you carried and delivered a baby, whether via caesarean or vaginally, drug-assisted or naturally, you're a real mum. In fact, if you didn't carry your baby and they arrived via surrogate or were fostered or adopted, you're a real mum, too.

If you worked hard to 'bounce back', bounced back with ease or never quite got back your pre-baby bod, you're a real mum. If you manage to shower, get dressed, apply some lippy and go to brunch, then you're a real mum. If you stay in your pyjamas all day and haven't washed your hair in nine days, let alone stepped out of the house, you're a real mum. And you're doing a good job!

For years, women have been shown an unattainable and unrealistic image of how they 'should' look in traditional media. The 'perfection' we used to see in magazines has now filtered into our daily lives through social media. Everyday mums are able to create personas of beauty and ease through curated feeds. Many, to be fair, Facetune and filter their photos, which puts unrealistic and unhealthy pressure on women who are comparing themselves to a person or image that isn't real. On the flip side, there is also a rise of 'real'—I prefer to call them 'raw'—Instagram mums, sharing an honest, warts-and-all account of mum life. While it is important to support and celebrate mums sharing uncensored realities, it's also important not to shame women who prefer to share a highlight reel of their motherhood experience.

When it comes to body image, I have noticed some instances where we have almost gone the other way by applauding women for not bouncing back and shaming those who do—whether they work hard at it or not—and that's not fair, either. Any judgment about a woman's body, regardless of their circumstances or physical shape, can have a negative impact on that woman. New mums are already in such a vulnerable place; we need to be lifting each other up, not tearing each other down.

The reality is some women will get their fittest, strongest body post-baby and others may never get back to where they started—for many different reasons. And that is OK. We should be focusing on accepting ourselves, accepting each other, appreciating what our bodies have done—their functionality—speaking positive words and showing gratitude to these vessels that have created life.

Just like it's OK to look tired and unkempt after having a baby, it's OK to look great and put together, too. If it makes you feel good, why not add a little makeup and take a selfie with a flattering angle and good light? You're still a real mum if you do that.

If you're happy to hang out in a topknot and trackies for the first three months (and beyond), you're still a real mum, too.

I didn't leave the house for four to five weeks post-baby. The last thing I felt like doing was taking post-partum pictures and dressing my cherub in outfits to take snaps. I tried to do it a few times and it was exhausting. My babies lived in singlets and were swaddled for the first three months of their lives—but that doesn't make me any more 'real' than the mum taking her three-day-old baby out to brunch wearing a Gucci smock to match her newborn's. Maybe they have help, maybe the baby is a great sleeper or maybe it took her four hours to get out of the house, but that was the one thing she wanted to do that day.

It's also OK to feel put together one day and then not shower for three days afterwards. I guarantee even the most glam mama on the 'gram has cried in the bathroom trying to settle a fussy baby.

If you carried and delivered a baby, you're a real mum. In fact, if you didn't carry your baby and they arrived via surrogate or were fostered or adopted, you're a real mum, too.

Just like there is no 'right' way for a woman's body to recover post-partum, there is no 'right' way for a mother to use social media. It's the comparison that drives women apart. The women with flat post-partum stomachs versus the ones with extra weight; the mum sharing sleeping pictures of perfectly dressed babies in flower baths versus the mum sitting on the toilet feeding her screaming baby.

I enjoy following both curated and 'raw' Insta-mum accounts. I understand that what people choose to share on the 'gram is a persona—a mere snippet of their lives.

The beauty of social media is that you can choose your experience. Fill your feed with accounts that make you feel good. If an overly Photoshopped bikini-model mum makes you feel bad, there's no need to criticise—jut unfollow her. A therapist once told me she never read the newspaper or watched the news because it was too disturbing. It made me understand that we can really choose our reality and what we experience in life. You can apply this to social media as well as your new-mum life. I can tell you now, as a working mother to a toddler, I barely know what's going on in the world news, but I know every word to 'Toot Toot, Chugga Chugga, Big Red Car'—and right now, that's working for me.

HEY, IT'S OK

BY SUSIE VERRILL, BLOGGER AND FOUNDER OF MILO & ME

Hey, it's OK if you've done nothing today. Your 'nothing' probably involved quite a lot of 'thing-ing' anyway.

It's OK if you only pretended to be enjoying playing 'boo'. You probably play it 36 times a day on average and, let's be honest, it's never a bloody surprise. They're right there!

It's OK if you teamed building a Lego kingdom with answering emails one-handed or emptying the dishwasher.

It's OK if you left your little one in the Jumperoo for longer than it's advisable. It's the one time you get to just sit. You don't ask for much; you just want to sit. And maybe treat yourself to a flick through Instagram or an extended yawn.

It's OK if you can't remember things or you're not sure what day it is. It's OK if you didn't hear what your other half said after they repeated themselves four times. It's OK if you get flustered. It's OK to feel overwhelmed.

It's OK if you can't remember if the pants you had on today are the same ones you were wearing yesterday.

It's OK if you really look forward to bedtime, only to spend half an hour scrolling through photos of the exact baby who's lying 20 feet away from you because you miss them. (Even if 20 minutes ago you were googling the minimum age for boarding school enrolment.)

It's OK if you hate the feeling of breastfeeding.

It's OK if your baby never manages to keep their poo inside their nappy.

It's OK if you get angry with your other half when he declares he's tired. It's OK if 20 minutes later you can't imagine loving anyone else because he made you a strong cup of tea without you asking, and he ignores the fact that your hair smells like dry shampoo.

It's OK if everyone else has managed to put on lipstick and casually wander to a farm with real-life animals and feed them with teeny-tiny bags of seeds they bought from the kiosk while you've not moved from your Lego Duplo-spattered living room for days.

It's OK if Ewan The Dream Sheep, baby massage, sleep training, dummies and everything else known to man hasn't helped you get your baby to nap without a fight.

It's OK to have one good day out of three.

It's OK if you let your toddler play with your iPhone all the time. Like, all the time.

It's OK if you don't get your baby changed out of their pyjamas when you're in a rush. They look cute anyway.

It's OK if you're giving off a chill vibe in public but are inwardly faffing and wondering why your baby keeps arching his/her back in the pram.

It's OK if you don't feel like having sex with your other half but give it a good crack anyway.

It's OK if you don't feel grown-up enough to be in charge of another human.

It's OK if you always lose your keys in your changing bag.

It's OK if you get to the cupboard and forget why you were there.

It's OK if you know every word to every song from The Wiggles, but have no idea what is going on in the real world.

It's OK if you don't do frequent date nights with your partner.

It's OK if your body isn't what it used to be.

It's OK if you declared you'd try not to become one of 'those mums' on social media and now you're juggling apps like some celebrities juggle plastic surgeons.

It's OK if you sometimes want to do a little ugly cry.

It's OK if you're dreading going back to work once your maternity leave finishes. It's OK if you can't bloody wait to go back, too!

It's OK if you cut up blueberries in case they're too big for your child's mouth, despite receiving constant mocking from family members about how your child will never live outside of a cotton wool-swaddled kingdom.

It's OK if you sometimes don't change the duvet cover because 'it was only a little bit of sick'. (It's dried now, anyway.)

It's OK if you'd rather do the worm over broken glass than endure teething (molars in particular).

It's OK if you like to keep it real by refusing to give your toddler the rest of your lemon muffin because it's bad for their teeth (and also you want it).

It's OK if you shout, 'Oh look! A plane! What do planes do?' by accident when you're out without your toddler because you've forgotten what it's like to not narrate everything.

It's OK to wonder how everyone on social media has such clean, monochrome houses when yours looks like a toy store mixed with a landfill site.

It's OK if you don't ever quite feel like you're doing enough, being enough or managing enough.

It's all A-OK.

GET IN THE PIC, MAMA!

Now that we are clear that 'real' mums come in all beautiful shapes and sizes, one piece of advice I would like to give new parents is to GET IN THE FRAME! Don't just take a million pictures of your baby or child; get in there with them.

Yes it's amazing to get a professional family session maybe once a year, but I'm talking about those everyday snaps that capture the in-between moments. No makeup, messy hair, in your pyjamas with your family. I guarantee they are the moments you will look back on most fondly.

And don't forget videos! I make it a habit to take ten–twenty seconds of footage most days. Just a few stolen moments to remember the sounds of their little voices, how they crawled, how they look at us, how we look at them. In one, five, ten or twenty years you won't care if you were 'camera ready', you will actually think you looked great and wonder what the heck you were worried about!

Taking family photos isn't always easy. I'm the first to admit the 'effortless' pic can take quite a bit of effort, but here are some tips to get you started.

1. Use natural light instead of a flash. A good picture is all about lighting.
2. Keep moving. Candid, in-between snaps turn out much better than staged photos. Even if the setting is staged, it's easier to get the kids to participate if they are just doing their thing. Jump in and interact with them, rather than get them to pose.
3. If you're like me and your eyes are closed all the time in photos, look at your kids rather than the camera. It's all about

the moments—and it's really hard to get everyone looking at the camera at the same time, so just act natural.

4. Keep clicking! A mama needs options. If you have fifty to choose from you are bound to find one or two that you like.

5. Don't critique yourself too much or worry about the angles—focus on the moments themselves.

6. A good preset can turn an average photo into a great one. Black and white is always a nice option, too.

7. Montage your video snippets and add music. There are many different apps to do this all on your phone.

8. If you don't know what to do with your hands then add some props. An ice cream, flowers or just holding hands are great options.

9. Don't forget Dad! Snap candid moments of your partner with the kids and make sure you get someone to take a photo of the whole family whenever you can.

10. Laugh and HAVE FUN!

TIMESAVING BEAUTY HACKS FOR TIRED MAMAS

Despite the fact that many mamas joke that parenting is a fast track to ageing, let me start by saying that this is not about how you look, but how you feel. For the most part, when we look like the best version of ourselves, we feel amazing. Yes, we're sleep-deprived, time-poor and have a to-do list that's a mile long, but that doesn't mean we don't want to look our best. They don't call it beauty sleep for nothing! So if you aren't getting any shut-eye, here are some tips to help you look like you are.

* Dry shampoo—I know, not exactly groundbreaking, as dry shampoo is a well-known time saver, but did you know dry shampoo is best used at night? It soaks up the oils while you sleep so you wake up with fresh hair. You can still use it in the morning, but tip your head over, spray underneath and wait fifteen minutes before giving it a good shake or blast with the hairdryer.

* Playing the part—if you haven't had time to get your roots done, you can change your hair part or, better yet, dust some eye-shadow in a similar shade to your hair colour along your roots. Not only will it blend the colour but your hair will look thicker, because let's be real—the only hair growth we get post-partum is on our chins and nipples!

* Use white eyeliner as a brow highlighter (above and below) for an instant eye lift. Yes, this works!

* Eye masks and face masks will be your BFF.

* Rose quartz face roller—leave it in the fridge to cool. It's great for under-eye bags.

* Get your eyebrows done. I can't stress this enough. Good brow work is like getting a mini face-lift. If you have time to get your eyelashes done too, that is my other tip for looking ready in the morning with minimal daily effort.

* To feel put together, sometimes it's as simple as getting a mani-pedi. If you don't have time to get to the salon, paint your nails while the baby sleeps. Use a fast-drying solution (there are now great options with fewer chemicals, too) or soak your freshly painted nails in a bowl of ice and water. It will help the polish dry faster.

* Get your products working double (or triple) time. Gone are the days when you had time to cleanse, tone, moisturise, prime, etc. Look for a tinted moisturiser that will give you hydration, coverage and SPF in one. If you really want to get serious bang for your buck, go for a BB or a CC cream as they give you all of that as well as nourishing skin benefits—win-win.

❉ Carry a lip balm and highlight stick in your bag for a quick 30-second freshen up.

❉ When nothing else is working or it's just one of those days, a red lip or shiny lip gloss with some dark sunnies is always a winning combination.

MINDFUL MAMA

After my first miscarriage, my friend invited me to learn Vedic meditation at her studio The Broad Place. I had always been open to meditation through my yoga practice and other holistic practices, but this was the first time I studied it on its own. I can say with confidence that it was a life changer. I was in a deep state of anxiety and grief from the unexpected loss and it was manifesting physically.

The effect of dedicating ten to twenty minutes twice a day to just sit and meditate was profound. It was such an essential tool in my fertility journey and without it, I couldn't have got through what was to come. I am grateful for the path I had to walk, as I was able to learn these skills that took me through a calm pregnancy and beyond. Even though I needed the twice-a-day practice to start, you don't have to dedicate that much time to it; even five minutes a day is better than nothing.

5 TIPS TO BRING CALM
TO THE CHAOS

BY JESSIE KAVANAGH, MINDFULNESS AND MEDITATION TEACHER,
YOGA INSTRUCTOR AND MAMA OF TWO

Motherhood is a joy-filled, exhausting, intense roller-coaster ride of demands, heart-swelling emotion and damn hard work. It's easy to let self-care slide way down the list of priorities, but we all know you can't fill from an empty cup. Meditation is a great way to give back to yourself and cultivate a clearer headspace to tackle all that life throws your way.

While adding meditation to your regular routine won't magic away the day-to-day chaos, it can help you deal with all the crazy. Think less stress/yelling/behind-the-bathroom-door breakdowns and more calm, control and actually being present in the moment.

Here are five simple strategies to help you create a little more calm among the chaos, straight away.

1 SCHEDULE A TIME
Schedule meditation time into your day just like you would an important meeting or doctor's appointment. The juggle is real as busy mums, and spare time doesn't just fall from the sky. Making meditation a priority might mean letting go of something else for a while. Start off small, even three to five minutes can make a difference.

2 CREATE A SPACE
Find a cosy spot at home that you can make your own. Somewhere you can relax and shut yourself away from the chaos. This could be under a blanket on your favourite chair, a soft pillow in the corner of your bedroom or, if all else fails, the quiet comfort of your car.

Our clever minds also begin to associate our special space with feelings of relaxation, making it easier to get the good vibes going each time we sit down to practise as well.

3 FOCUS ON THE BREATH
Tune into your breath before you begin your meditation. When you take a moment to shift from fast and shallow breathing to slow and controlled breaths . . . whoosh—in comes the calm (just like magic)!

At some stage during your meditation practice, your mind will wander. Don't worry—it's completely normal. When this happens, use your breath as an anchor. Draw your focus back to the present moment, back to the sensation of each breath as it flows in and out.

4 GET GUIDED

If sitting (or lying) down in silence feels a little intimidating, try using a guided meditation. There are heaps of great apps (such as Insight Timer) and YouTube videos out there that don't cost a cent to use. You can also pop on some relaxing music if guided meditations just aren't your jam.

5 THROW OUT THE RULEBOOK

On days where actually sitting down to meditate just isn't going to happen, try to make a meditation out of normal everyday tasks like washing the dishes, folding the laundry or taking a shower. Be fully present in the moment and focus on your breath.

Make your meditation practice your own. Sit up, lie down, do it while you're on the toilet if you have to—whatever works for you. There is no such thing as a perfect practice; there is no wrong or right way to get it done. So make it work for you.

Meditation is a habit that can take time to build, so be patient with yourself throughout this process. It doesn't always feel easy; you won't always be left feeling blissful and serene. Just like motherhood, some days it can feel damn hard . . . but if you make it part of your regular routine, it just might change your life.

STYLE HACKS

Contrary to what we may have been conditioned to think, becoming a mother doesn't have to mean losing yourself (or your style).

In saying that, becoming a mum can definitely mess up your style game. This was one of the driving factors behind me creating Not So Mumsy; I found a huge gap between the fashion blogs and magazines I followed pre-baby and the new 'mummy blog' world of pureed banana I was now in the midst of. I couldn't find anything for modern mamas like me who weren't quite ready to hang up their J'Adior slingbacks but had nowhere to wear them.

In my pre-baby life I worked in media. It was more creative than corporate, so I could have fun with my daily outfits. I would add a killer heel to dress up my jeans and a tee, or add studded boots and a leather jacket to dress down a pretty dress. I found the style transition into pregnancy dressing pretty easy. I loved dressing my pregnant body, but dressing a cute bump is very different to dressing a post-partum body—one that is likely to continue to change—and this is where it took me a little while to find my style mojo.

In the first few months with a baby there's nowhere to really go. Maybe for a walk or to the park, but nowhere that requires anything fancier than activewear, and definitely nowhere that requires heels. I would often stare at my 'in between' wardrobe and pull out the same leather leggings (reflux appropriate—so practical) and an oversized tee pretty much every day. But after a few months, I needed a little more from the style files, so I decided to focus on accessories. I feel this is the best 'new mum' style hack. Adding a fab bag, sunglasses, earrings, a headband, some jewellery or cool trainers would make me feel kind of stylish, and still a little bit like the 'old me'. And if you mix up the accessories, no one will notice you're actually wearing the same outfit. Again.

HOW TO GET YOUR STYLE MOJO BACK
AFTER BECOMING A MUM

BY STYLIST ROSIE MCKAY

Ah, motherhood. It makes your heart overflow, steals your boobs and—let's face it—at times it steals your sanity, too. But if there is one thing I vowed it would not take away from me, it's my style. Despite that fact, even I can attest that after my second babe, Maia, was born, I subscribed to the Lycra-all-day-every-day school of style for way longer than I should have.

Don't get me wrong, I love activewear, but I feel best in it when I can actually work out. Otherwise, on those really testing days when nothing goes to plan, it just feels like a reminder of the workout that never got done—and quite frankly I'd rather not be reminded of that fact!

As a working mum I quickly realised that dressing for the way I wanted to feel, in clothes that make me go 'mama's still got it' is so empowering and completely shifts my mindset.

So, if you feel like you've lost your style mojo, it might be time to hang up your leggings (until your next workout, that is) and start making your way back from mumsy to not so mumsy (pardon the pun). Not sure how or where to start? Here are my top tips for getting your style mojo back.

DE-CLUTTER

If you don't feel good wearing it, or it no longer suits your body shape, it's time for it to go. Here's how to kick-start your de-clutter:

* Go through your entire wardrobe and make three piles: keep; donate; repair, tailor or dry-clean.
* Reorganise everything you want to keep by style and then by colour. For instance, I have sections for tees, tops, shirts, dresses, skirts, pants and jackets, and then I arrange them by colour.
* Drop off your donations, repairs and/or dry-cleaning items. Sometimes an alteration like lifting a hem or removing a sleeve will breathe new life into an existing piece.

SHOP SMART

It's really easy to buy things on a whim just because 'it will do' or you saw it on Instagram and you don't have time to shop. After de-cluttering I would advise to start rebuilding your wardrobe with intentional purchasing. Start with what I like to call a 'core wardrobe', which is a tight edit of pieces that mix-and-match into a variety of looks that won't date easily. These pieces allow you to create a series of effortless go-to looks that will take you from running errands to park hangs, soccer practise and beyond. A blazer, stripy top and leather pants combination is one of my all-time favourite looks—I just switch up the shoes depending on whether I'm heading out the door to an appointment or to a play date with friends.

Stick to neutral colours like white, black, grey, nude, navy and red. They all work together and don't date easily. But, in saying that, don't be afraid to add some personality to your look by choosing pops of colour, striking silhouettes or statement accessories that suit your personal style.

Just don't go overboard buying too many trend-driven prints and colours because you will end up with a wardrobe full of pieces that won't work together. Also, where possible, try to buy an entire outfit that you love. Knowing you have a complete outfit that works together takes the guesswork out of getting dressed when you're strapped for time!

DRESS FOR YOUR SHAPE

There is no denying that your shape changes after having kids. Even if you go back to the size you were pre-baby, you will notice your clothes will sit differently. My best advice here is to stop worrying about size and just dress to flatter your shape. If that means buying a medium instead of a small or a size 12 instead of 10 because it looks better, just do it.

I have a mix of size ranges from small to large in my wardrobe. I buy the size that works best for the way I want to style the outfit I'm wearing. Focus on buying silhouettes that highlight your best bits. Love your shoulders? Show them off with off-the-shoulder tops. Adore your waist? Highlight it with high-waisted bottoms or belted outfits.

UPDATE YOUR HAIR AND MAKEUP

It's amazing how a new hairstyle or a colour change can instantly make you feel like a million bucks. Updating your image is the perfect finishing touch to your new wardrobe. You know what they say—a change is as good as a holiday—and given you have kids and that holiday could be a long time coming, going a shade lighter or darker sounds like a bloody good idea!

chapter nine: navigating career and motherhood.

I hope you understand that
I'm doing this for mama (me),
   but I'm also doing it
for you—because of you.
   I don't want to just
   tell you that you can
do anything or be anyone.
   I want to show you.

Contrary to common belief, having a baby actually ignited my search for passion and purpose in my career. I have had some amazing career highs over the past few years and I haven't done those things despite being a mother; I have done them because I am a mother. How powerful is that?

In my pre-baby life I worked as a hostess at a high-end NYC celebrity restaurant. I met Sarah Jessica Parker and lost Alec Baldwin's coat. I spent months in Africa bottle-feeding lion cubs, I cycled across Cambodia volunteering in orphanages, I modelled in the UK and I travelled through Central America with the Panamanian Latino surf tour. In between these adventures, I had quite a successful media career, working almost ten years in newspapers and TV. While pregnant with my son I was the marketing manager for an iconic BBC children's channel, which prepared me nicely for that 'new mummy daze' where I spent many hours staring at *Peppa Pig* long after my baby had left the room.

I had a full, adventurous life and thought the height of my post-baby 'adventure' would involve a trip to the sandpit, and that leaving my baby sans nappy for twenty minutes would be as 'living on the edge' as #mumlife got. I was convinced that real adventure wouldn't have a place in my new role as a mama; and in the beginning, that was probably true.

I also thought that I had already hit my career peak. I believed that going back to work

173.

post-baby would just be for supplementary income and an excuse for a little bit of 'me time'. (Both of these are valid reasons though, of course!) I wanted to throw myself into my new role of 'mum' and I had no interest in climbing up a corporate ladder, but I also didn't want to lose myself completely. That's how Not So Mumsy was born.

I was prepared for the lifestyle changes that motherhood would bring. I knew my priorities and perspective would change, but I wasn't prepared for the changes it made to my inner world. It might sound crazy, but becoming a mum gave me the confidence to trade my comfortable nine-to-five for my passion project. It ignited the fire within me to start my side hustle; it gave me perspective to not just settle, but to live my best life. To show my children, not just tell them that they can be anything or anyone.

Yes, there are limitations, but you can keep the adventure in your life (if you want to, that is). I can now say as a mother of a seven- and a two-year-old that some of my greatest adventures have happened since becoming a mother. When I was in my early twenties I was scouted for a big modelling agency in Sydney and in London. I never took these opportunities because I had confidence issues and body-image issues. I didn't believe in myself and knew it wouldn't be the best decision for my mental health. It was never really my dream to be a model, but I did often wonder what I missed out on and I was hard on myself about it. I would never, in my wildest dreams, have thought that in my mid-thirties I would start landing campaigns with Australia's biggest brands. That I would be the face of Bras N Things for Mother's Day, that I would be flown to New York for Maybelline, that I would be featured in many magazines and even on a cover. All of this was because motherhood gave me the confidence to believe in myself. Doing these jobs now is so much richer because they have so much more substance; there is a story behind them. I'm doing them all not despite being a mum, but because I *am* one.

You see, you don't really know how you're going to feel until after you have your baby. This goes for work, too. You may think you will want to jump straight back into your career, but find you'd rather stay at home. Or you might think you want to stay at home, but find that after the baby comes you can't wait to get back to the grind. Or you may just find a whole new side hustle or career in motherhood. There is no right or wrong here, and there is so much grey area.

The way we work is changing. There are so many more options than just being a 'working mum' or a 'stay-at-home mum' (SAHM). While it's true that motherhood can in many ways limit career progression, there are also ways in which it can actually be beneficial, and provide new and different opportunities. The lines between office and home are becoming increasingly blurred. There are so many ways to work that are making it easier (and harder!) to be a boss mama. What I have come to learn is that we needn't limit ourselves to old ways of working, and that embracing flexibility can help our working lives.

This new liberation of choice around our decision to work has meant some women feel shamed for wanting to 'simply' stay at home and nurture and nourish their children. After all, we're told we can 'have it all', right? Well, I think most of us can agree being a SAHM is hard work. In fact, at times it's harder. I know I've been there counting down the minutes until Daddy's home!

You may think you will want to jump straight back into your career, but find you'd rather stay at home. Or you might think you want to stay at home, but find that after the baby comes you can't wait to get back to the grind. Or you may just find a whole new side hustle or career in motherhood. There is no right or wrong here, and there is so much grey area.

Before kids, many mums think being a SAHM sounds amazing as you get to hang out with your children all day long. And for many mothers, they're happy and content with this lifestyle. But for others, once the reality of being at home all day with the kids kicks in, many mums yearn for that sense of independence, of having a life outside of their children.

I have been a SAHM, a side hustle working-from-home mum and a full-time working mum, and I can tell you that one is not easier than the other. If you do have the luxury of choosing between going back to work or staying at home, just make the decision for you—not because of what others might think or say about you, or what you think society expects you to do. Make the decision for you and your family.

FINDING *YOUR* PASSION

BY FREELANCE WRITER AND EDITOR JESSICA BOSCO

Motherhood is, without a doubt, one of the most profound, life-altering journeys you will experience as a woman. Nothing can prepare you for becoming a mother and how it will change you. And the change is profoundly different in everyone. Some women find that becoming a mum ignites a switch in them and they immediately know what they need to be doing with their lives, whether that's quitting their job to stay at home with their kids, leaving their job to finally turn their side hustle into a reality or forging on and rising up the corporate ladder of their dream job. Whatever it is, they just know.

But then there are those of us who feel a little lost. In motherhood, you go through all of these profound changes and feel like a completely new person. But when you return to your old job, or find yourself home alone with the baby, you can feel lost. Like you're in limbo, living two parallel lives and never feeling quite right in either

of them. You know your old job is no longer fulfilling you, or you know you want to do something more than stay at home with the kids, but you just don't know what (yet) . . .

These eight questions, written by recruitment expert and director at Top Talent Executive, Tracey Lane, are designed to help you find your passion, purpose and path.

Tracey, a mother of two, knows first-hand what it feels like to need to take a step back and revaluate what is important to you. 'I've done a lot of soul-searching myself over the past few years, and I initially wrote this list of questions when I was at a point where I needed to re-evaluate what I was doing'.

So whether you're at the point where you want to make a change, or you're not even sure if you need to, or if you like to start off each year with a little self-evaluation, here is what you need to ask yourself. Take your time with the questions and be truly honest with your answers. You might be surprised by what you come up with.

1 What are your three favourite topics to discuss? What could you talk about for hours on end?

2 Ask five people who love you and know you best what they believe you would be amazing at doing . . . no judgements, just listen!

3 Think of five people that inspire you (or people that you envy), either locally or globally. Who are they and what is it about them that sparks something within you?

4 What are you doing when you are totally 'in your element' and time just disappears?

5 If you were granted a wish that would ensure you make money from your creativity and talents, and you could not fail, what would you do?

6 What do people ask you for information on and advice about? In which areas are you deemed to be a little fountain of knowledge?

7 What do you like to spend your time reading, viewing, watching or learning about?

8 If you didn't need to make money and you had an endless fountain of funds, what would you do to keep yourself busy every day? (By this I mean after you have travelled the world, bought your dream car and house, etc.) What would you want to do day in, day out?

MANIFESTING

I remember having an argument with my husband during the infancy of Not So Mumsy. He was travelling for work for months at a time and we were arguing about time management—namely how I had taken a step back to be a SAHM for him to prioritise his new business for years, but I had no time to work on mine. We had just returned from three months in NYC where he was setting up distribution for his company, and he said something along the lines of, 'When Not So Mumsy pays our rent and funds our family to travel overseas, we can talk.' I turned around and said with so much conviction, 'I guarantee it will.'

I had so much belief in what I was doing that I even surprised myself. I worked around his travel schedule and the baby, usually between 9 p.m. and 1 a.m., with purpose and passion to create something that would sustain and fulfil me.

I knew it would be a success. Not so much from a monetary or 'recognition' point of view—that definitely wasn't the driving factor—but in terms of building a community of like-minded mamas and a platform that could give back. That's how I define my success because that's what I set out to achieve. I posted the following quote by writer Julia Cameron on my personal Instagram account just before I launched Not So Mumsy, and it still holds so much truth for me: 'When we do what we are meant to do, money comes to us, doors open for us, we feel useful, and the work we do feels like play to us.'

Just for the record, Not So Mumsy has since taken my family to California, London, Greece, Paris, NYC, Dubai, Bali, Byron Bay, Palm Cove and Melbourne— and my husband is my biggest supporter.

Many of us are living our lives based on someone else's beliefs of what we should be doing, instead of doing what makes us happy. Once you understand and truly believe you can do anything you set your mind to, it is liberating.

'The Universe will match whatever vibration you put out. And you can't fool The Universe.' I just read this quote in Jen Sincero's book *You Are a Badass: How to stop doubting your greatness and start living an awesome life*, and it resonates with me so much. I am a huge believer in the power of manifestation. That if you have a clear vision of what you want, put in the work and do good things, it will come to you.

Last year I declared it would be our 'year of travel'. I wrote it on my goal list and within two weeks we were invited to California by Disneyland, and I secured a partnership with a global brand to fly around Europe. This year I was in the kitchen with my husband and said, 'I feel New York in my bones, and it would be nice to do my first trip without the kids.' That very afternoon I had an email asking me to audition for a role in NYC for Maybelline.

I didn't even dare to dream of these things as a new mother, but each year I worked hard and set myself clear goals. Now, I realise the only thing that was holding me back was myself.

WORKING FROM HOME

For many new mums the idea of working from home has become the Holy Grail. Laptop in one hand, baby wipe in the other and world domination while you're still in your pyjamas. Surely this is what they mean by work–life balance, by 'having it all', right? Well, not necessarily.

Whether you're running your own business, starting a side hustle or have a flexible job you can do remotely, working from home as a mum definitely has its perks. It's flexible, there's no commute and you can work around your kids . . . but it's not all pyjamas and slippers. It can be quite isolating and lonely. It can also be really difficult to separate home and work, which means it's easy to get distracted and not get much work done, or, on the flip side, it's easy to work around the clock with no clear downtime.

Of course, there are those who would trade The Wiggles and mashed banana for a cuppa and chat with Karen from accounts in a heartbeat—like anything in life there are pros and cons for both scenarios.

I worked from home for four years and although I missed the daily social interactions with my workmates, I loved the freedom and flexibility. But there are a few systems I had to put in place to find that balance between freedom and productivity.

* **Passion.** The key to motivation is to work on or create projects that you love. If it doesn't feel like work, you will happily spend hours doing it.
* **Stick to a work schedule.** If the kids are in school, make sure you block out a certain amount of time just to work. Don't worry about the dishes or that 'one' load of washing. You can do those things when the kids are home. If you work with kids at home, identify the best time you can get a couple of hours done without any distractions. Maybe it's sleep time or when your partner gets home. On the days when my son is at home my work starts at 6 p.m., as this is when my husband can take over parenting duties.

* **De-clutter your workspace.** If you create a beautiful space to work in, you will be happier to spend time there. If you de-clutter your desk you will de-clutter your mind, which will lead to more productivity.
* **Don't watch TV on your lunch break.** I have fallen into the *Dr. Phil* vortex . . . before you know it *Entertainment Tonight* is on and then it's a slippery slope to school pickup and the afternoon is gone.
* **Put down the phone.** Social media is a time trap. One minute you're liking Michelle's breakfast and the next you're twenty-nine-weeks' deep into your ex's ex's profile. I give myself an hour in the morning and an hour at night to catch up on the Insta-world.
* **Meditate and stretch.** Research shows us that meditation can improve concentration and productivity. I always take twenty minutes before I start work to meditate and five minutes to stretch and regroup every couple of hours to prevent those computer strains and refresh the brain. Also, try and eat your lunch outside in the sun!

FOUR STEPS TO MAKE THE TRANSITION BACK TO WORK EASIER

For those returning to an office or out-of-home workspace, it can be a daunting transition for a number of reasons. But there are some things you can do to help yourself adjust to your new normal.

1. Hash out the logistics. Organise childcare a little while in advance if you can and do some trial runs.
2. Bring your baby to work before you start. This is good for you, but also good for your workmates, as they will see your new reality and focus.
3. Find your tribe of other supportive working mums.
4. Get rid of the 'mum guilt'. Most mums will go through a 'want to quit' phase, but give it a little time and, if possible, don't make these decisions in the early months of working-mum life. If it's been a few months and it's really not working for you, see if you can work from home or reduce your days. If you want to start your own thing—give it a crack! You've got this!

WHAT NO ONE TELLS YOU ABOUT
GOING BACK TO WORK PART-TIME

THE WRITER HAS CHOSEN TO REMAIN ANONYMOUS

In my life before my baby I was pretty ambitious. I had a clear direction of where I wanted to go and I was well on my way there. Then I fell pregnant, and suddenly I was into the whole nesting thing, and I was so happy to finish up work and begin my new life as a mum. Secretly I was thinking that maybe I wouldn't go back to work at all; maybe I'd be a SAHM . . .

Flash-forward a year and I knew the SAHM life was not for me—not at this point, anyway. I knew I needed something of my own, and I still wanted to work. Plus, I knew I would regret it if I didn't go back and give it a go. Add to that the bills stacking up (renovating your house while on maternity leave and relying on one income is not a great idea). Weighing up our options and the exorbitant cost of day care, I decided that part-time was the way to go, and off I headed back to my old job.

Naively, I really thought it wouldn't be a big deal. I thought to myself, I'm still me. My workplace is open-minded and is happy to accommodate me going part-time. This will be great. It didn't exactly go according to plan. But not for the reasons I expected.

I was lucky in that, for me, the easiest part was bubs. He settled into day care (almost) seamlessly, so that was one major weight off my shoulders.

Unsurprisingly, however, after a year of singing The Wiggles and having one-sided conversations with a human blob, I was pretty rusty at my job and it took my brain a while to switch back into gear. It took a lot of smiling and nodding for me to feel competent again.

I realised I had changed after all. So much. I felt like suddenly I'd been thrown back into my old life but I was a completely different person—and those two worlds were now colliding.

Some people return to work and breathe a sigh of relief, feeling like they're back where they belong. But that wasn't the case for me. This sudden identity crisis struck me hard, and trying to find where I fit in now really threw me.

You find yourself navigating things like all the new staff that have come along and got comfortable while you were gone.

To you, they're the newbies, but to them, you are. Then there's the drama that all too quickly sets back in; the office politics— it's exhausting. And as any mum who has returned part-time will tell you, you start to try and overcompensate and go above and beyond because you don't want to be seen as the weakest link. But despite everything you do, you often will be seen that way.

Before I got pregnant I had laid down some serious groundwork; I had been earmarked for a promotion that was apparently coming 'any day now', but then as my bump grew, I quickly came to realise that the baby was coming before any promotion was. So, with nothing on paper, I left with a, 'We'll call you when the job gets approved.' That call never came, so when I returned part-time, I was in the same role.

But what I naively didn't realise was the effect that being part-time would have on my standing within my team and the company—and my ability to get ahead.

I didn't get the promotion when the restructure finally happened months after my return. Instead, I got a new title. When I asked why I missed out on the role I had wanted, they told me the person who got it had really stepped up that past year (when I was off, you know, having a baby) and that the role really needed to be full-time.

And while I don't begrudge the person who did get the role for getting ahead, it's still a bitter pill to swallow when you know that job would have been yours had you not taken a year off and if you didn't now have a kid.

My pride took a huge dive after that, but the good thing is, when you're a mum you learn to put things into perspective. Once upon a time I would have been overwhelmed by my devastation, whereas now I can brush it off much easier. I made my choice to work part-time, but that doesn't mean it doesn't still hurt.

But it's not just the big moments like team restructures that you need to prepare yourself for, it's also the everyday things: the meetings you're left out of, the emails you're left off 'because you're only part-time', or when your desk gets moved to the end of the row beyond the most junior member 'because you're hardly ever here'.

If there's one piece of advice I can give, it's to ask your boss about what you returning part-time means to them. For some people, part-time is the perfect option to stay in the game while being able to take a step back from the pressure and responsibility. But if you're there to still work hard and get ahead, then you need to make sure you're in a company that will let you do it. It's all well and good letting you go part-time, but if that then means you're pigeonholed and overlooked for promotions and unable to thrive when that's what you still want, then maybe it's not the right workplace for you any more.

Q&A with
emma isaacs

BY FREELANCE WRITER AND EDITOR JESSICA BOSCO

Whether you're a SAHM mum, a working mum, a 'mumpreneur' or a dreaming-of-taking-your-side-hustle-to-the-next-level mum, sometimes we all need that extra kick to get out there and do the thing we've been putting off (or stop doing the 3453 things we've been trying to unsuccessfully juggle).

Meet Emma Isaacs. If you haven't heard of her then you would have definitely heard of her company, Business Chicks, which is the largest network for women in Australia.

After starting her first business at just eighteen years of age, and now with twenty years of business experience—and five kids—under her belt, Emma has released her first book, *Winging It*, which is full of advice and tips that draw on her own experiences in business and motherhood, as well as advice from those she's met along the way.

*AT WHAT POINT IN
YOUR CAREER DID YOU
BECOME A MUM?*
I became a mum for the first
time when I was in my late
twenties and I'd had my first
business for twelve years.
I think my business really
equipped me to be a mum,
in terms of working really
quickly and productively,
and how hard I hustled
really helped when I started
running a family and trying
to fit in as much as I could.

*WITH SUCH AN
ESTABLISHED CAREER,
DID YOU FEEL LIKE
MOTHERHOOD CHANGED
YOU OR THE PATH YOU
WERE ON AT THE TIME?*
Because my whole identity
was about being an
entrepreneur, I did find
it hard to adjust a little
bit, because that was so
ingrained in who I was, and
all I knew was running my
own companies. I tried to
keep on that path as much
as possible and not deviate
from it. I was 29 when I
became a mum, and you
have a lot more energy

then—my foot was on the
accelerator and if I took it
off it would have made it
that much harder to get
back. So I did make a
conscious decision to keep
driving my career as much
as possible and that worked
for me. This might not work
for everyone, though—I
didn't take much maternity
leave the first time around.
But the benefit of being
established in my business
and financially secure was
that I was able to make my
own decisions and choose
where I wanted to put my
time. I feel very grateful that
I started so young and set
myself up so that when the
babies came along I had a lot
more choice available to me.

*YOU'RE A MUM OF
FIVE NOW, WHICH IS
AMAZING—DOES IT
GET EASIER EACH
TIME OR IS IT JUST
CONSTANT CHAOS?*
Going from one to two was a
massive adjustment, you feel
like you've just sorted it out
and then you throw another
one in the mix. But having

had five now, I think the
biggest jump was possibly
two to three—when they
start to outnumber you!
I'll never forget the moment
we had our third baby. The
nanny went home one night
and all three started crying
and we just looked at each
other and we said, 'I don't
know where to start!' It was
basically which one do we
like the best [laughs]? But
now it's just all relative.
I had three of them with
me yesterday and it was
so easy, but you just don't
know what you're capable
of until you're capable of it.

*YOU TALK A LOT ABOUT
WINGING IT, BUT ARE
YOU A 'FLY BY THE
SEAT OF YOUR PANTS'
TYPE OF PERSON DAY-
TO-DAY, OR ARE YOU A
METICULOUS PLANNER?*
I'm a weird combination
of being quite OCD but
also being very calm and
very, very relaxed. The
name *Winging It* came from
personal experience. I've
always been doing things
without knowing how to do

them; I started my company without any experience, I parent five kids without any experience, I wrote a book without any experience. We're all so hell-bent on getting things right, and getting all our ducks lined up in a perfect row, that we forget to just take it easy, have fun and try new things. It does come back to having self-belief and backing ourselves, but ultimately we need to not take ourselves too seriously. I think it's hard when we see people on social media and we think they have it all together. We have to just come back to what we want out of our lives, to identify what's precious to us and just focus on that.

Also, we need to have more fun. I see people stressing out that things aren't working out how they're meant to, but there's no blueprint for that. There is no blueprint for life that says you have to do things a certain way. The message is to just lighten up and have a go, even when you don't have all the answers.

We have to just come back to what we want out of our lives, to identify what's precious to us and just focus on that.

IN YOUR BOOK YOU HAVE A SERIES OF QUESTIONS WE SHOULD BE ASKING OURSELVES. ONE, IN PARTICULAR, STOOD OUT AS A GOOD REMINDER TO US ALL: 'HAVE I DONE ANYTHING WORTH REMEMBERING LATELY?' Absolutely. Not only can it serve you in your personal life, but it's also such a powerful tool in business. These are the things that get you remembered. I recently played a practical joke on my editor, and she wrote me an email back saying, 'Oh don't do that, you're going to give your poor cardigan-wearing editor a heart attack.' And then just this week after the book launch I had a beautifully wrapped cardigan to give to her as a thank you for all our hard work together. She was blown away that I had remembered, and she's probably going to go home and tell her partner/mother/friend, and it might get them talking about me or the book—or it might not—but I don't do it because I want something from it. These are the things that make us human. They're so important, and we forget that life and business can actually be that simple. It's just about really seeing people and seeing what they like or maybe what they're struggling with. And that's the way we've really built our business over the years because kindness is where it's at and there are ways to stand out, for sure.

WHAT ADVICE DO YOU HAVE FOR MUMS WHO ARE KEEN TO 'WING IT' BUT ARE AFRAID TO TAKE THE LEAP OR DON'T KNOW WHAT THEY WANT TO DO?

Well, firstly, it's best to try something on the side before you throw in your financial security. But you need to really have a long, hard think, and it might be difficult, but think about why you want to do something. Do you just want to do it because everyone else is doing it? Do you want to do it because you want to make more money?

Everything comes back to the 'why'. If you want to spend more time with your kids, you need to ask whether a small business or side hustle will actually give you that. Be super-clear on why you're doing something and then try and find

There is no blueprint for life that says you have to do things a certain way. Just lighten up and have a go, even when you don't have all the answers.

something that fits around those needs.

And then it's a matter of checking in with yourself and asking, is this actually working? Because it may not be. I see a lot of small business owners putting themselves through a lot of hardship and financial stress just because they think they want to run a business. Being an entrepreneur is one of the toughest gigs you

could ever do, and we do glorify it, which can be kind of unhealthy, but that's why I admire people who share how hard it actually is to run a business.

Finally, network everywhere! I talk about this a lot in the book but you really need to start with an audience. If you have an audience already, then think about what product or service might benefit them. It's better to attack your business from a 'What's my audience?' basis and go from there, rather than try to find people to buy your product, which is reversing the way a lot of people look at a business. It's all well and good to say you've got to have a passion and love what you do, but business is business, and for it to work you have to make more money than you spend—that's 101—and a lot of people get lost in that. If you don't need the money and can go and follow your dream, then great, but most people need to make a living from their business, so you need to think about the 'why'.

WHAT IS THE BEST ADVICE YOU'VE BEEN GIVEN?
My first company was a recruitment business and I now run the largest network for women in Australia, and the common denominator of both of those businesses is people and relationships. I think that no matter who you are, a lot of success comes back to how well you can navigate relationships and how well you can build your network. There's a saying, 'Whenever you need a relationship it's too late to build one,' so let's just say, for whatever

reason, tomorrow you're in a difficult situation and you need to raise capital for your business. It's very, very hard to start from the absolute get-go and to find people who are willing to fund you. But if you've been kind to people, you've kept in

No matter who you are, a lot of success comes back to how well you can navigate relationships and how well you can build your network.

touch and done a lot more for others than you've done for yourself—and done so selflessly—you never know when your network is going to need to be activated. So you cannot underestimate how important it is to be kind—and really work on that network.

WHAT MESSAGE DO YOU WANT PEOPLE TO TAKE FROM YOUR BOOK?

I hope people are inspired to know the time isn't ever perfect, and that we can't wait for the right timing or the right opportunities. We really have to chase them down, and I want people to feel like they're empowered to make their own decisions and call the shots. I think people often look at other people and think, *They've got a better life*, or *They're more attractive/smarter/ wealthier*, etc. We look at them and think they can do more because of that. But really, it's within all of us to make powerful decisions and decide what kind of life we want to have. The book debunks a lot of those myths that we all have— and it just proves that anything is possible if you get your mindset right and surround yourself with the right people.

chapter ten: travelling with tots.

You will never regret showing your kids the world.

Not So Mumsy.

There's a running joke among parents who travel that we don't go on holidays. We just look after our kids in different cities. I know what you're thinking—you can barely survive a trip to the shops with your 'spirited' offspring, let alone a long-haul flight in a confined space surrounded by strangers. Then there's jet lag, new surroundings, language barriers, lack of routine, no backup or chance of a break . . . hang on, why do we do this again?

Oh yeah, because some of our most treasured memories have been made exploring new countries and cultures. To be fair, some of our most horrendous parenting days have also been on the road (that 26-hour commute from Greece to London, I'm looking at you!), but you can't have the rainbow without any rain!

After travelling to twelve countries and taking more than fifty flights with children between the ages of three months and six years, I can assure you travelling with tots is manageable—most of the time. And even when it's not, it's 1000 per cent worth it.

There will most certainly be a point (usually mid long-haul flight) where you'll curse the idea and promise yourself the next time you share an aircraft with them will be when they're old enough to share a bottle of shiraz and chuckle along quietly to *Love Actually* with you.

Then, when you finally get there (or maybe before you leave?), there might be a mega meltdown at customs (highly recommended for a fast pass), a change room disaster, a spilt drink or a badly timed 'poonami' . . . but most of these mini-disasters happen at home, too, so you may as well change up the scenery, right?

Transit days can be hard, but there was also that (one) time where I managed to watch my first entire post-baby movie and had someone bring me a cup of tea—so I'd say it's worth the gamble.

In all seriousness, the tough bits are usually only a small part of the trip, and with some careful preparation and the right attitude, travelling with tots really can be the time of your life. I would take 100 long-haul flights just to see the delight on my little son's (Nutella crêpe-stained) face when he saw the Eiffel Tower light up for the first time, and 100 more to see my kids play under a tree in a tiny Greek town that had been on my vision board to visit for years.

Of course, every child and every situation is different, but here are some of the things I've found most helpful when travelling with children.

PLAN & PREPARE

The first thing to do before you begin planning is to shift your mindset and expectations. I spent many years of my pre-baby life living, working, volunteering and travelling. I was determined to keep that sense of adventure after I had kids (insert eye-roll here), but yep, you guessed it, the reality is it's a totally different experience.

I can tell you with confidence that a five-day wilderness trek along the Burmese border, eating slugs and camping with hill tribes has got nothing on trying to keep a one-year-old buckled in on a plane when the seatbelt sign is on. You can't control what may or may not happen, but you can control how you react and how it makes you feel. An open mind and a relaxed attitude are always a good start.

Keep your itinerary light and loose. The less expectations and pressure you place on yourself and your travelling tot(s), the more flexible you can be in the moment. Plan one activity per day and allow for some downtime and free play in the afternoon. If it's going to be hot, choose accommodation with access to a pool so the kids can play while you (try to) relax.

WHERE TO GO

Remember that relaxing beach holiday destination you loved before co-creating? Yeah, well it's not going to be so relaxing with tiny human(s) in tow. It may be fun, it may be memorable, but it probably won't be relaxing. Chances are you need a holiday after your holiday.

As long as you know this going in, you can minimise the potential pitfalls by being prepared—whether that means lining up babysitters in advance so you can have a night out, or just a child-free afternoon by the ocean. Do the legwork in advance to ensure the destination or resort is able to accommodate your needs.

WHERE TO STAY

As much as I love staying at a hotel or resort, since becoming a second-time parent I now favour self-contained accommodation for longer stays. Particularly for the first few days in a new time zone after a long transit.

We booked into a London hotel after a 30-hour trip from Sydney. The kids' jet lag was out of sync, which meant the hyper child would keep the sleepy child awake and vice versa. It also meant I didn't get one wink of sleep for the first five days and was often confined to the bathroom for 4 a.m. 'game time' with my then thirteen-month-old baby. Surprisingly, not so much fun, but lesson learned! Separate bedrooms make it easier for the whole family to get maximum sleep.

There is also more room for the kids to play with new toys and games, as well as a kitchen to prepare healthy meals, which saves costs from dining out. There are even specific booking agents that focus on and cater to family homestays all around the world.

HOT TIP: DINE AT NOON

Dinnertime with kids can be overwhelming at the best of times. There's nothing more frustrating than trying to enjoy delicious cuisine while chasing a toddler and having a baby throw spaghetti in your hair. So unless you want a highly stressful encounter with a side of indigestion, have your family meal at lunchtime when the kids are in better spirits. Lunch menus also tend to be less expensive than the dinner versions, so it's a win-win.

GETTING THERE

Whether flying, driving or riding the rail, make it a rule to have no rules on travel days. This is one of the most helpful travel tips I have come across. Your ultimate goal is to arrive at your destination alive and sane, and for many, a relaxed 'anything goes' attitude may just help you get there. Screen time, lolly bribes (although too much sugar on a plane can have the opposite effect), little presents—whatever it takes until you arrive at your final destination.

FLYING

We all know the anxiety of boarding a plane with tots in tow. I mean, those little buggers are so unpredictable. Even when they are behaving we are in a constant state of anxiety trying to pre-empt what could be touched, thrown, broken, tantrum trigger-worthy or all of the above. It's also not helpful when you have child-free adults eyeballing you as you board the plane with thirty-five bags, a toddler hanging off your back and a baby in the sling.

When it comes to flying with babies and toddlers, I like to use my general parenting motto: 'prepare for the worst, and you'll be pleasantly surprised.'

The general consensus is that between the ages of zero to seven months is a great time to fly with babies. The biggest perk of this age is that they don't move! Stationary babies are easy(ish) babies. They pretty much just eat and sleep—and they fit in the bassinet. The downside is they also cry, which is not so fun. Also a jet-lagged baby can be intense—but if you have a non-sleeper it could be a blessing in disguise.

If you have an eight-month-old to a two-year-old child—strap yourself in. This age range is the hardest to fly with. The combination of busy hands, short attention spans, confined spaces, tantrums, wanting to get into everything—did I mention tantrums? And don't get me started on trying to wrestle a nappy onto a fifteen-month toddler in a tiny wobbly cube while trying not to breathe or touch anything thanks to Mr 22C.

The real challenge is that before twelve to eighteen months they may be too young to be distracted by screens—oh the horror! But alas, it can and it will be done. I can assure you we've all stared longingly at the emergency exit while trying to restrain a one-year-old thirty minutes into a fifteen-hour flight. We've all given the 'this is literally hell on earth' nod to other toddler parents on the 357th lap of the plane, but we all agree that it is worth it.

8 TIPS FOR FLYING WITH KIDS

1. Choose a night flight for a flight that's more than eight hours.
2. The sling/carrier will become your BFF on board. Especially if your baby is too big for the bassinet.
3. Don't let crawling babies on the ground. Once they know they can go down they will want to keep doing it.
4. Pack individual nappy wipes, clothes and sock bundles in separate bags so you are not bent into a pretzel rummaging through your nappy bag.
5. 'Busy bags!' Pack a small bag of surprise gifts/toys for toddlers to unwrap when they become unsettled or bored.
6. iPads are life when it comes to flying with toddlers. Limit screen time the few days before you fly so it's a novelty.
7. Have that glass of wine/beer/spirits with dinner—and don't watch the clock countdown.
8. Sunlight and running on some grass is the best cure for jet-lagged kids.

Whether flying, driving or riding the rail, make it a rule to have no rules on travel days. This is one of the most helpful travel tips I have come across. Your ultimate goal is to arrive at your destination alive and sane, and for many, a relaxed 'anything goes' attitude may just help you get there.

PACKING

The first rule of packing is don't pack everything! I have to constantly fight the urge of the last-minute panic shop where I want to buy the whole pharmacy 'just in case', but then I remind myself that wherever we're going, children live there!

Most destinations have a delivery service for things like bassinets, high chairs, strollers, toys and even nappies. So you only really need to focus on packing what you need while in transit.

Start preparing to pack a few days before you travel. Keep a running list of things to take, or put items out on a table or dresser as you think of them.

Use a nappy bag with a waterproof lining and a shoulder strap. Take an extra outfit or two for your baby and an extra shirt for you in your carry-on bag. Pack each of your baby's outfits in its own zip-lock bag so you don't have to hunt around for tiny socks, shirts and so on. Also, don't pack with your toddler or baby in the same room. They will unpack as you pack.

THE ULTIMATE PACKING CHECKLIST

* **Nappies**—you can never have enough! To be safe, pack one nappy for every two to three hours you'll be in transit.
* **Change mat**—I use one that holds a nappy and some wipes so you don't need to carry the whole nappy bag into the change room. This is especially helpful when changing in the plane toilet.
* **Blankets/swaddles**—bring a few. You'll use them to lay your baby on, cover your baby, cover yourself if you're nursing, protect your clothes from messy burps, as a pram canopy, plane seat cover—the list goes on . . .
* **Plastic/disposable bags**—carry a variety of sizes for soiled nappies and storing wet clothes and blankets. You will also need them for medicines.
* **Travel-size nappy rash creams** and **baby body wash.**
* **Wipes**—you'll need these for bottoms, faces, hands—basically everything. I seriously don't know what I did with my life before wipes.
* **Hand sanitiser**—I use a natural essential oil spray and spray down the

whole area on the plane/bus/car. It's perfect to use without water.

* **Dummies!**—and dummy chains if your babe leaves them on. We left with eight and were down to one by our flight home—it was like juggling gold!

* **A few of your baby's toys**—maybe some new ones for older babies, too— the surprise factor might encourage them to play with their new toys a little longer.

* **Clothes, socks and shoes**—one to two outfits per day is a good guideline. Don't forget a sun hat.

* **Feeding utensils, bibs and baby food**—if your baby's eating solid foods.

* **Formula or water**—if appropriate.

* **Breasts**—if, like me, you exclusively breastfeed, this is super-easy.

* **Healthy snacks**—for you as well as older babies.

* **Nightlight**—comes in handy to keep the room lighting soothingly low during middle-of-the-night nappy changes/feeds.

* **Medical essentials**—baby pain reliever and supplies for minor injuries.

* **Vitamins for Mama**—don't underestimate a good multivitamin for a tired travelling mama.

* **Phone/camera/chargers!**—you're making memories after all—you're going to want to document them.

* **Essential oil rollers/blends**—for older babies I had a calm/teeth blend and a cough blend. Please note babies under three-months-old shouldn't use essential oils—refer to guidelines for older babies.

* **Sling/baby carrier**—this is a lifesaver! It makes walking those aisles (and waiting around for the plane) much easier. And hands-free!

* **Car seat**—if you purchase a plane seat for your baby, some airlines will allow you to bring your own car seat. Now I know I was just banging on about packing lightly, but if you have a good car sleeper and/or your child is too big for the bassinet, this could be your ticket (to a movie at least!).

* **Collapsible pram**—a travel stroller that fits in the overhead luggage compartment is possibly the best travel hack. It makes life so much easier! And don't forget your stuff, too!

TRAVEL TIPS FROM FIVE OF *OUR FAVOURITE* FAMILY TRAVEL WRITERS

BY KAREN EDWARDS, A MUM OF TWO, SENIOR NURSE AND TRAVEL BLOGGER AT TRAVELMADMUM.COM

It's a common misconception that travelling with kids is really difficult. I'm a firm believer in being prepared to make the journey as easy as possible. That's generally the obstacle to the end prize—enjoying the destination! Once you get to the destination I find it's so much easier. I follow my favourite acronym I recently coined: SAS. It's a little similar to the internationally recognised SOS sign for help. SAS stands for snacks, activities and sleeping aids. If you are well prepared with these three things for kids of all ages from baby up, you are likely to have a relatively hassle-free journey.

Don't overdo it with packing is my second biggest family travel trip. There is no need for all the kiddie paraphernalia or a tonne of clothes. Only bringing what you are most likely to use will make it as hassle-free as possible. I say no destination is off limits. You don't need kids' clubs and all the facilities. I find when taking kids to any beach, mountain, lake, new city or town that they find new things that stimulate all of their senses. Last but not least, just do it. If you're thinking of booking a trip but have some hang-up about it not being manageable with the kids, don't let it stop you. Your kids will thank you later.

BY GEORGIE WATTS FROM THE WINDOW SEAT

If you loved travel before kids, there's no reason not to love it once you have a family. The trick is to manage your expectations. Travel with children will not be the same as travel pre-kids, but this is not to say that it can't be enjoyable, relaxing and rewarding. When your kids are little, you may feel limited by feeds or naps, but the good news is it gets easier the more you do it and the older the kids are. We travelled to Italy with Wolfie as a three-month-old baby, and it was a disaster. We were disappointed that it was so difficult, but we learned so much.

Currently, what works for us is exploring and sightseeing in the morning, and pool time in the afternoon. This ensures there's something for everyone.

BY NARELLE BOUVENG, A TRAVEL WRITER AND MOTHER OF THREE. W: ALITTLEATLARGE.COM

Kids call it a surprise kit; I call it a survival kit. Here's what you need to pack in your surprise/survival kit:

* Three Chupa Chups for older kids (perfect to provoke an extended period of quiet and/or to release ear pressure).
* A sheet of stickers (the backs of seats and windows are perfect sticker boards and they are easy to peel off quickly).
* Wet wipes—my kids would spend hours cleaning the seats and windows (weird, I know), and it eliminates all germs in the process.
* Two-minute noodles—a last resort if plane food doesn't cut it.
* Small jar of Vegemite—you can always find bread in any country for a sandwich, and I may have used it as finger paint on the odd occasion, too . . .
* A favourite book and a new one (surprise), colouring book and pencils (surprise) and a notebook (even little kids can play tic-tac-toe).
* A toy from home and a new one (surprise).
* Kids' painkillers.
* Lavender spray—it's great to cleanse stinky air and is also a sleep-inducer, calmer or pillow spray.
* A cloth nappy—it has multiple uses, wet and dry.
* A pillowcase—this works as comfort and is able to cover or conceal anything grotty. It also works as a makeshift laundry bag and as super-quick storage if you have to clean up quickly and run.
* Earplugs for all members of the family. If all else fails, just plug them in, smile and ignore.

BY JADE GIOVANNETTI FROM LUXURY FAMILY TRAVEL BLOG WOLFANDMOSES.COM

My number one travel tip when travelling with kids is to relax and just go with it! Easy, right?! It can be daunting, but I promise despite all the bumps that travelling with kids can throw at you that it is absolutely worth it.

Travelling slower and more mindfully is really important when kids are involved. Spending more time at each destination, getting to the airport earlier so no one has to rush, etc. are all things that will help you (and the rest of the family) be able to be more relaxed and therefore enjoy it more.

Don't stress about following the exact same routine that you have at home. By all means keep it loosely the same, but don't worry if a nap time is spent in the pram while sightseeing or if bed times are later than normal so that you can dine out at night (you never know, it might mean a sleep-in the next day!).

I am not going to lie, travelling with children can be hard at times. There is guaranteed to be tears (from possibly everyone!), mess and sleeplessness. Even though it's not always easy (parenting never is), the special experiences you will get to share together as a family, the memories you will make and opening the kids up to the world around them makes even those more difficult times easily forgotten. Just try it!

BY EVIE FARRELL FROM TRAVEL BLOG MUMPACKTRAVEL.COM

Adventures together as a family are some of the best gifts you can give your kids. Yes, travelling with children takes a bit more planning and it's not as easy as the simple days of setting off alone or as a couple but, in my experience, the rewards far outweigh the challenges. Spending time together brings you closer and you'll learn much more about your children when the barriers of routine and responsibility are stripped away.

My daughter Emmie and I had our first overseas holiday when she was four months old, and we've had many adventures since. I've watched her grow into a little girl who is confident when meeting people and being thrust into new situations, who is strategic from learning how to plan on the road and who is accepting of others from being exposed to cultures and religions during our adventures. Most importantly, when travelling we have precious time together to explore, learn about the world around us as well as learn about each other. It's time together that can't be bought and can't be replaced.

The bonds forged by travelling together run deep. Sharing new experiences as a family, learning side-by-side and conquering the hard yards together brings everyone closer. It gives so much joy and creates incredible memories to talk about for years to come. When you travel with your kids, you give them the world, and sow those seeds of open-mindedness, acceptance and adventure—and what could be more rewarding than that?

The bonds forged by travelling together run deep. Sharing new experiences as a family, learning side-by-side and conquering the hard yards together brings everyone closer. It gives so much joy and creates incredible memories to talk about for years to come.

chapter eleven: can we really have it all?

'BRB. Just trying to excel in my career, maintain a social life, drink enough water, exercise, text people back, stay sane and be happy.' It's a real balancing act and that doesn't even take into account keeping your kids alive! So here is my shout-out to the tired mamas! To the working mamas, the stay-at-home mamas, the single mamas, the mama hustlers. There has never been a better time to be a woman. The sky is the limit and it's our time to shine.

But the pressure to do it all while maintaining our role as a primary caregiver is not easy. The juggle is real. Can we do it all? Do we really want it all? As I write this chapter in a hotel room on the second night away from my family, I guess my personal answer is 'yes, we can', but not necessarily at the same time.

I love what I do. I'm so grateful and proud of the work life I have created, but I'm also overwhelmed most of the time. I feel guilty, I feel pulled and I feel stretched. I struggle to fulfil the competing roles as a mum, wife and aspiring boss lady.

Just having a family is a juggle. Add a career, side hustle, friends, fitness and something to satisfy our soul—it's easy to burn out. High-achieving women everywhere are maxed out and overwhelmed—and a lot of the pressure comes from ourselves. We live in a culture of comparison. One that glorifies 'busy'. Are we doing enough? Are we doing it well?

Ironically, I even put pressure on myself to 'slow down and be present'. I fantasise about being the #slowliving mama who shops at the farmers' market and bakes superfood brownies, but in reality (in this season, anyway) I am that mum burning around the supermarket on a time trial, apologising as my toddler pegs linguini, my school boy begs for (highly processed, definitely not vegan) treats and I skim read (but rarely answer) texts and emails pinging on my phone.

Somehow I think I've become addicted to this fast-paced life. I want to grab on to the opportunities. They fulfil me and give me an identity outside of 'Mum', but other days I want to throw it all away and just be Mum. The push–pull is real. So is the pressure to attain the elusive 'balance'. I think it's much more attainable to work on a 'blend'—a fluid one at that, which changes with different seasons. What is important to me is that family is always my priority.

Even if my daughter knows the Uber Eats bag means 'num' and I'm not cooking as much as I used to because of my current workload, I'm not beating myself up about it. I'm doing the best that I can for my family in the current circumstances. Our children will love us regardless. I'm sure most mamas can relate to the meme that goes: 'It's either me OR the house who are going to look tidy today. Not both. Never both.'

I'm very passionate about the idea that having kids can enhance your opportunities or capabilities, rather than limit them, but there is absolutely a limit on how much we can juggle at the same time. We have an incredible ability to multitask, but we have to understand that one or more of the things we're trying to juggle probably won't be done to a great standard. If I'm full steam ahead on the work front, my house will look like it's been robbed, dinner has been delivered on a motorbike and I won't have responded to any texts for a week. If I'm living my best 'mum life' by cooking dinner every night, helping out at school and getting to tutoring, soccer and ballet sessions on time, then work emails will get missed and I won't have time to exercise. For me, the key has been to drop 'perfection'. Done is better than perfect. Some things will be done at 50 per cent and that's OK.

Why are women
**expected to work like
they don't have children**
and
**mother like
they don't work?**

— SHANNA HOCKING

FIVE CELEBRITY MAMAS SHARE *THEIR TAKE* ON THE MODERN-MAMA JUGGLE

Eschewing the desire for perfection, we find out how these five celebrity mamas juggle career, health and happiness.

TERESA PALMER
Actress, writer, model and film producer

I think perhaps society puts unfair pressure on women to 'do it all' but that doesn't mean balancing it all isn't possible for those who want that. I have a desire to be a great mum, have a successful acting career, a blogging career, be philanthropic, have a wonderful relationship, be a good friend and be rooted in a deep spiritual practice. To me, that's the Holy Grail, and why not strive to find balance in all the things we want to achieve? This doesn't mean I will achieve it, but at least I know what my goals are and I have an idea of something to strive towards and for me, that keeps me focused. That's just my path and it might not be someone else's. I know so many women who are content with being a great wife and mama and they're not so focused on work, and that's just beautiful too. I may only be successful on my journey some of the time but I never put pressure on myself, and most importantly I never listen to what anyone else thinks I should and shouldn't be doing, especially around societal pressures.

What it really boils down to is not being in a state of comparison with anyone else, cultivating self-love and acceptance of what is, and really doing the work to figure out what kind of experience we want from life.

JAIME KING
Actress and model

I was not meant to be a stay-at-home mum because my acting and creative heart need to express in that way. Although it is very difficult not sleeping and working crazy hours, I do what I can to keep him [my son] close so that I am still raising him as my mother raised me. Even though she did not have to go to a workplace, raising three kids at home is just as hard! I believe that it takes a village, and we are in an interesting time where we have been taught that we should be able to do it all and have it all. Have kids, a great career, a great relationship, a healthy life, etc. and be some kind of one-woman army. That is not only impossible, but it's also totally unfair to place those expectations on us as women. I do not believe that men struggle innately with this as women do because women always have to prove themselves in the workforce as equals. Though, of course, many loving and hardworking fathers face these dilemmas and I want to acknowledge that as well. Throughout history, people always relied on their families, tribes, friends and loved ones for assistance. So when I am judging myself for not being able to juggle everything perfectly, I try to remember that we are not supposed to! I remember that even though all of my family lives far away from me, I can ask a friend to come over and play with him [my son] so I can hop in the shower or go to the doctor's. Our children will love us no matter what, if that is the love we are putting out there to them.

When I am judging myself for not being able to juggle everything perfectly, I try to remember that we are not supposed to! Our children will love us no matter what, if that is the love we are putting out there to them. — JAIME KING

TAMMIN SURSOK
Actress and singer

My mantra for myself and other mothers is: 'You can have it all, you just can't have it all at the same time.' The minute I accepted that, my whole life changed. I spent a lot of time in the beginning as a new mum feeling so guilty that I would leave Phoenix to go to work . . . and then feeling equally guilty that I wanted to work when Phoenix was around. You just have to be present in the moment and be grateful, and not expect everything to be perfect all at once.

EMMA ISAACS
Entrepreneur

We can have what we choose. So for me, my life only consists of two things: my business and my family. I am a lousy cook, I am a pretty woeful friend at times and I do not work out, apart from lugging my kids' toys up the stairs eighteen times a day—that's my gym! My entire life at this moment is being in my business and with my family. I believe we can have what we choose—we just can't choose too many things.

I don't think any mum with a young family has the capability of ticking every box. It's how we go about bringing mental health back into our lives. How can we ask ourselves if we're enjoying what we're doing, and if we're not, what can we change? Do we need to get more help, do we need to ease back a day a week in the office? It's about having the conversation with ourselves and identifying if this is working for us. We need to be more kind to ourselves and know that no one can have everything. Do the things you do well, and don't choose too much.

MEGAN GALE
Model and entrepreneur

Modern motherhood and the pressure of trying to do it all and have it all can be a slippery slope. Personally, I think we need to cut ourselves some slack.

On one hand, I do love the whole 'boss lady' movement—it's great that women are urging each other to be the best mum, wife, businesswoman, friend, etc. they can be. But I also feel that, as inspiring as that is, it is also adding pressure on us to load up on what is often an already very full plate.

As women, we have a tendency to look at others and compare ourselves, but I think, especially where motherhood and juggling additional priorities are concerned, we really need to steer clear of all of that comparison and judgment and sometimes just be.

It can be overwhelming trying to juggle it all, to have it all and I am a big advocate for stepping away to disconnect to reconnect and, sure, to be inspired and driven, but not to the detriment of your own health and at the expense of quality time with your loved ones and yourself.

That's how I manage all of my lot in life. If I didn't, I would get overwhelmed by it all and really come undone. I know myself well enough to know when to step back from work and step into family, or to step away from being Mum and connect back into my relationship and give that some TLC. By having that self-awareness and listening to myself, I shift my attention to where it needs to be for that hour or that day.

I've come to the conclusion that our health and happiness are what truly matter most. Much more than being it all and having it all.

We need to be more kind to ourselves and know that no one can have everything. Do the things you do well, and don't choose too much. — EMMA ISAACS

A FINAL NOTE

There's a quote by an unknown author that says, 'One day you will tell your story of how you've overcome what you are going through now and it will become part of someone else's survival guide.'

I really feel like this book wrote itself. It's the culmination of six years of using my platform to connect women with each other and to share their stories, as well as share my own.

I have been part of a virtual village. I've seen the power of what mums supporting mums looks like. We have laughed, we have cried. We need each other's stories; we need our modern mama village—even if it's a virtual one.

These shared stories and perspectives show us that we all do it differently—and that's OK. We don't need to be told how to do it and we don't need to be judged on how we're doing it. We actually need support because we are in it. We are living this roller coaster and it is hard, but it is beautiful. What a blessing to experience motherhood, even on our toughest days, even when things don't go to plan. It may very well break you, but then it will make you.

These stories show we can celebrate the power of motherhood, but still admit it's hard. We can master it all one day and then fall to pieces the next. We can be tough but vulnerable, tired but strong. We can celebrate motherhood, but still retain a sense of who we are as women.

Yes you're a mum, but you're still you. You can still be you. You don't have to lose yourself in motherhood. In fact, you can actually find yourself—your passion, your happiness, your purpose.

You can find the confidence to be who you want to be. Not despite being a mother, but because you are one. You just need to believe you can.

To my wonderful contributors—you have been my village, my support. Thank you for trusting me to pass on your stories, perspectives and experiences. We're Not So Mumsy together.

ACKNOWLEDGEMENTS

To my Not So Mumsy community, I'm so honoured to have you here. We have shared stories of love and loss, our beautiful moments and our toughest days. We have been each other's village. Thank you for sharing your stories and for allowing me to share mine. I have received countless emails and messages from women thanking me for helping them, particularly through their fertility journey. Truly it's all of you who have helped me through some of the toughest moments of my life. It's these shared stories that keep us connected.

To my contributors: Jessica Bosco, Phoebe Shields, Pippa James, Rachelle Rowlings, Nicole Highet, Lauren Heffernan, Amberley Harris, Anita Heiglauer, Colleen Temple, Kelly Müller, Leila Stead, Keren Moran, Danielle Maloney, Susie Verrill, Jessie Kavanagh and Rosie Mckay. Thank you for allowing me to share your words, and for giving a voice to so many. To my travel mums: Karen Edwards, Georgie Watts, Narelle Bouveng, Jade Giovannetti and Evie Farrell for reminding us that we can keep the adventure in our lives. To the high-profile mamas: Jaime King, Megan Gale, Teresa Palmer, Tammin Sursok and Emma Isaacs for inspiring us with your authenticity. To Carmen Yeates, the only photographer who has captured the true essence of our family and Paula Kuka for your talented illustration and concept.

To my OG 'renegade mothers' group': a bunch of first-time mums who had no clue about anything. Those weekly catch-ups got me through my first year and you were the first people who listened to me yabber on about launching Not So Mumsy.

To the team at Murdoch Books: my publisher, Kelly Doust, for trusting me to share this message. My editor, Justin Wolfers, and freelance editor, Ally McManus, for your ease to work with and being gentle with me when the deadlines nearly broke me. To Jacqui Porter from Northwood Green for bringing my vision to life—you have captured the essence of Not So Mumsy in such a beautiful way.

Most importantly, to my family: Mum, thank you for allowing me to share a part of your story. You have survived more than most could bear and continue to teach me the true meaning of unconditional love. My husband: for years, I stood beside you as you created your dream, thank you for standing beside me as I create mine. The months of late nights and days away writing; you mastered the school drop-offs, school lunches, dinners, baths and bedtimes like a boss. I wouldn't have been able to finish this without you—you are a true partner in every way.

Finally, my children: the loves of my life. My children in my arms and my children in my heart. You are my reasons. You have taught me more about life than anyone else. You have given me my purpose, ignited my passions and helped me to find who I truly am. I am so blessed to be your mama.

Marcia xo

ABOUT THE AUTHOR

Not So Mumsy founder and editor Marcia Leone lives in Sydney with her hubby, soccer-obsessed seven-year-old son and two-year-old daughter.

Alternating between a holistic lifestyle and eating Nutella from the jar while watching *The Real Housewives* from everywhere, Marcia is an organic-loving germophobe with a healthy dash of OCD. If she were a drink, she'd be an activated green juice with the occasional nip of vodka.

A lifestyle journalist turned marketing and events manager, Marcia spent a decade of her pre-mama life working in newspapers, magazines and television. While pregnant with her son, she was the marketing manager for an iconic BBC children's channel. Despite her adventurous pre-mum life, Marcia found her true purpose and passion in motherhood, and took the brave leap in trading her comfortable nine-to-five for her own little passion project, Not So Mumsy.

What started as a website to fill the gap between fashion blogging and traditional 'mummy blogs' quickly became a community of like-minded mamas. Now, six years later, it has grown into a globally renowned, award-winning fashion and lifestyle destination for the modern mother.